For years Thyra Bjorn's fans have clamored for the truth behind the fiction and here it is at last—a story of joy and tragedy, of hard work and difficult decisions, of family crises and personal sacrifices that made it possible for her to succeed as a wife, mother, writer; to become, more than an author, a friend to the millions who have read and responded to her books.

Above all, here is a portrait of a woman who dared to dream and saw those dreams come true.

This Is My Life

THYRA FERRÉ BJORN

PILLAR BOOKS NEW YORK

THIS IS MY LIFE

A PILLAR BOOK
Published by arrangement with Holt, Rhinehart and Winston

Pillar Books edition published May 1976

ISBN: 0-89129-137-7

Copyright © 1966 by Thyra Ferré Bjorn

Printed in the United States of America

PILLAR BOOKS
(Harcourt Brace Jovanovich)
757 Third Avenue, New York, New York 10017, U.S.A.

This book is lovingly dedicated
to our two daughters so dear to our hearts
Shirley and Carolyn

FOREWORD

This book speaks for itself; I don't think it needs an explanation. It is record of happenings since I became an author, but it is more than that; it includes the little things surrounding a life, my own life. As I have written this record, I have lived my life over again. I have laughed and cried over it, and I have realized more than ever how blessed I have been to have a reading public which has accepted my writings in such a fine way. I feel a deep sense of gratitude to my publisher, who has been willing and eager to accept my simple writing and to the staff of Holt, Rinehart and Winston, who are as excited and happy as I am when a new book is born.

I feel that, through this book, my readers will know me better; and strangely, as I wrote it, I seemed to know myself better. I hope that it will touch a flame in some writers' hearts and that they, too, will dare to dream their dreams and find that at the end of each there hangs a miracle.

Longmeadow, Massachusetts, January 30, 1966.
With my good wishes to all,

THYRA FERRÉ BJORN

❧1

The day had started wrong. It was one of those days that happen to a housewife every so often. There was even a strange feeling in the air, an ominous feeling that something terrible could easily happen.

Christmas had just passed with all its fun and excitement. As usual, the house had been filled with gay company. My sister Margaret from Philadelphia had decided to stay with us over the New Year's holiday; and on this particular day, December 30, 1954, I was giving a small dinner party in her honor.

As a rule I am a good cook, but this day the magic touch was gone and whatever I undertook seemed to turn out wrong. Of course it wasn't my fault; it was the day that was to blame, and I was thinking just that as I put the roast beef in the oven. It was a beautiful piece of meat, and at least nothing could happen to that. But I was mistaken! When I put the meat in the oven, I turned the heat up high so it would brown quickly. Then I went upstairs—for a few moments, I thought. But I got involved in things and forgot the meat. A feeling of alarm struck me when an unpleasant odor drifted up the stairs and smoke began to fill the house. I hurried downstairs as fast as I could, took the meat from the oven, and placed it on the back step with the door wide open so the smoke would go outside. My heart sank. Now I would have to wash the roasting pan, scrape the burnt portion from the roast, and start all over again.

The day was damp, and to make things even more miserable it had begun to drizzle. As I stood there in the doorway, looking up at the heavy, gray clouds, a big dog suddenly dashed out of nowhere, and quick as a wink he stole my roast from the pan. For a moment I was too stunned to think; then my first thought was to run after the dog. But what could I have done if I had caught him? That moment seemed like the end of everything. Wasn't it enough that the meringue on my lemon pie had fallen and that the dough I had set for my butterscotch rolls refused to rise and that everything else had gone wrong that morning? Now, on top of all that, I was minus the main course of my dinner. My budget was low in those days and I didn't have the cash to go out and buy another roast. Tears began to roll down my cheeks as I told Margaret of my predicament.

"Now all I can do is to make Swedish meatballs," I sobbed, "and my guests will never know they were supposed to have roast beef."

My sister put her arm around me. "And you make the best Swedish meatballs in the world, Thyra. We'll all like them just as much as a roast. Your dinner will be tops, as usual."

But I wasn't so easily reassured.

"Oh, it won't be the same at all, but thank you for your compliments. I'll have to make the best of things and pray that tomorrow will be a better day."

I wiped away my tears and tried to smile. Soon we were on our way to the market to buy the best hamburger my purse could afford. It was when we returned from our shopping trip that the next thing happened. As we hurried from the driveway to the front door, we realized that the drizzle had turned to a steady rain. My sister had the key to the house and I carried the groceries, not just hamburger but ice cream in case the pie was too weepy and bakery rolls to replace my nonrising dough.

I can still see Margaret placing that key in the lock and turning it a few times unsuccessfully.

"You must have given me the wrong key," she said finally. "This one doesn't open the door."

"It should," I said and then I gasped. A horrible thought began to form in my mind and a sinking feeling filled me. My sister had been the last one out. . . . "Margaret," I whispered hoarsely, "when you shut the door, you didn't push—"

"If you're thinking what I think you are, I did." She smiled a faint smile. "When I leave my house, I know the door is locked if I've pushed in that little button on the inside."

"But ours isn't that kind of button. I have no idea why it's there; but when it's pushed in and the door is shut, nothing in the whole world can open it from the outside."

"Maybe the woman who lived here before wanted to keep track of her husband. If the button were pushed in and he tried to sneak in at three o'clock in the morning, he'd have to ring the bell. Do you think that's why it's there?"

"I don't know why it's there," I snapped, "but there's no one inside to open it now and we have all those meatballs to roll and it's late already. What in the world can we do?"

It took us an hour to get into the house. We tried everything, but all the downstairs windows were locked and had stormwindows on. We even borrowed a ladder from across the street, but neither of us was brave enough to climb as high as the upstairs windows. As I was descending from my second attempt at climbing, a small boy gazed at us from the sidewalk.

"Are you locked out?" he asked, looking very amused.

"Yes, we happen to be just that!" I said curtly.

"Why don't you call the police?" he asked.

I'd never thought of that, but it seemed like a good

idea and I hurried next door to use the telephone. The police arrived without delay; and since they were experts in just this sort of thing, they had us inside in no time. We were wet from the rain and cold from the wind, but there was no time to think of that. We hurriedly started the meatballs.

When the guests arrived, there was no trace of misfortune. The table looked lovely and everything turned out pretty well after all. My meatballs were excellent; there was a festive feeling in the dining room with laughter and fun at the dinner table. But as I look back to that evening now, I know that it was at that hour my new life began. My whole world was to be changed. But I had no forewarning of this as I said to my guests, "It's so soon after Christmas that if we were in Sweden, I'd have at least three kinds of dessert to offer you."

Just at that moment the telephone rang. My younger daughter went to answer it, and a moment later she was back in the dining room.

"It's for you, Mother," she said. And seeing the look on my face, she continued, "I couldn't have them call back. It's long distance and urgent. It's your literary agent from New York."

I excused myself from the table and hurried to the telephone in the hallway, wondering what my agent was calling me for at this time of the day. Perhaps to tell me she could come now for that visit she not been free to make at Christmas. That would be nice, I thought hopefully as I picked up the receiver.

The next few minutes were the kind that you wish would last forever. The words spoken from the other end of the telephone line changed my whole world, and suddenly I felt as though I were floating on a big, fuzzy cloud high up in the sky. We talked for a long time, but I remembered few of the words we said. Only one big golden sentence engraved itself deeply on my mind and heart. My manuscript had been accepted by Rinehart & Company of New York. My dream of becoming an author was to be fulfilled. It was at that moment that my head began to spin. A thrill like that very

12

seldom happens more than once in a lifetime. I had asked my agent to repeat what she had said. She did so, and I knew then it was true. I had not heard wrong.

Long after my agent had hung up I still sat there with the telephone in my hand, staring out through a small window high up on the front door. *Papa's Wife* was finally going to become a book. A book that would have many pages and a number on each page. There would be a jacket enclosing all those words I had written and under the title would be my name. What a wonderful, wonderful thing to happen at the end of such a trying day!

The rain had stopped now. There were stars in the sky, and I sat there looking at one big shining star. It was the most beautiful star I had ever seen.

Finally, when I did not return to the dining room, my guests and family came out into the front hall and found me sitting there. For a few moments I didn't realize their presence; I was still floating on that beautiful cloud. My state of mind was hard to describe in words; suddenly all was well with the whole world and there was such peace and contentment within me, a feeling that I had reached the goal that had been eluding me all my life.

My sister told me later, "It was wonderful to see you sitting there looking like that. Your eyes sparkled with the light of a thousand suns. We knew right away that something very special had happened."

I know that that light filled me all that night. We went back to the living room to sit and talk. I had forgotten about our dessert and no one else remembered it either. It was much later that I realized I had never served any. I told my guests about my book, the manuscript that had taken me five years to complete, a little bit of what it contained, and I answered their many questions. Everyone rejoiced with me.

"We'll always be able to say, years from now when you are a world-famous author, that we were with you when it all began," said one of my friends, taking me in her arms.

It was a night that would never be forgotten by those of us who experienced it. A day that had begun in disaster, had ended in triumph, light, and glory.

It was very late that night when we went to bed, but I could not get to sleep. How could I, when there was so much happiness in my heart that I was almost bursting apart? From the time the telephone call had come, I had known that the tears welling up within me had to be released; but there had been no chance to cry during the evening. Now the tears were still there, begging to be freed. After my husband was asleep, I quietly left my bed and went to the chair that stood in front of the typewriter table. It was there I had created my story. I knelt by the chair, buried my face in my hands, and let the tears come.

I cried for a long, long time, tears not of sorrow but of joy, victory, and triumph; and then I prayed, thanking God for my success. This was a sacred moment, one of the greatest of my life.

"God," I prayed, "I have thanked you for this wonderful gift of writing that you have planted within me, a talent so rare and beautiful. Now I ask You to keep me humble and make me always remember that this talent is a gift from You. Now that success has come, I could so easily become proud and forget Your goodness to me. I don't want that ever to happen. I want to write more than anything else in life; but if I should become proud and think I am better than others because I can write books, then, God, take my talent away. Keep me grateful and helpful to others and let me always remember that it was You who gave the gift to me. Amen."

When I returned to bed, I felt years older, as though in a few moments I had grown out of the me that used to be. The restlessness was gone and there was tranquillity and peace and confidence. I could see life ahead of me as a straight, wide road with the sunlight shining on it. Soon I fell asleep and I slept until late the next morning.

❧2

How well I remember New Year's Day, 1954! That was the day my manuscript was completed, the last sentence written on the final chapter. The last touch had been the retyping after it had been corrected by my very capable literary agent. To me it looked beautiful. It had never looked like this before. I likened it to a handmade suit that had come from the tailor who. had pressed it to perfection.

My English had been faulty because I had not had very much schooling in America and the tutoring I had had in Sweden in earlier years I had forgotten long ago. When I wrote, I never let myself become fenced in with mere words. It didn't matter to me if they were spelled correctly or if a sentence structure was wrong. I just let the words come. Joyously, from a full heart, they were put down on the white paper in my typewriter. If I couldn't think of a suitable word, I often made one up. It was my way of writing. The correcting my agent took care of and she looked out for all those little things without changing my style or story. She was wonderful and God-sent. She was a special blessing that I had accepted with the rest of the gifts I had received from God. I did my typing slowly with two fingers, but the speed was right for me. As I set my own tempo, I learned to create through my fingers.

How strange that an agent had come my way when I had never really looked for one. It had happened at a conference in historic Northfield, Massachusetts, where I had been sent to represent my church. As always in those days, when I traveled away from home, I took my writing with me. One night it as announced that there would be a fun period the next evening, an amateur hour when everyone was asked to share her talents. I decided to dramatize my story, "How Mama Got Papa," the first chapter of my book. It would be a good opportunity to see how people reacted to my stories and I was anxious to try it.

But that night I had a strange dream that troubled me long after I awoke. I had only a faint recollection of what the dream had been about, but there had been a voice calling to me and it seemed to ring in my mind. "Don't read your story tonight!" the voice had said. "Don't read . . . don't read."

At first I tried to laugh it off. After all it was just a dream and I shouldn't let it bother me. But there was something different about this dream. Though I tried to ignore it, a restlessness came over me, with the result that I withdrew my name from the evening program and informed my roommates of my decision. They looked very disappointed.

"But we've been looking forward to your story," one of the ladies told me. "It isn't fair to let us down now."

"I know what we'll do!" exclaimed the second lady. "If you don't read it to the group, you'll have to read it to us. Let's go out to that ice-cream parlor on the country road. There are never many people there. We can sit in a quiet corner and enjoy your story."

It seemed fair and I happily agreed. Right after dinner that night we got into my car and drove through the countryside. The place was almost empty, so we found ourselves a corner. We ordered ice-cream sundaes and as I was about to begin my reading the ladies spotted two others sitting at another table.

"Why don't we ask them to join us?" I suggested. "They're from the conference; I've seen them there."

We did, and I began my story to an audience of four. There was much laughter and interest; I could tell I had captured the ladies, and their faces revealed a certain gaiety and relaxation that I always found when I told of the strange romance of my Mama and Papa.

When I was through, I was showered with compliments.

"I like that story!" one of the new ladies exclaimed. "It's so charmingly funny; you really should get it published."

"I wouldn't know how to go about it," I said.

"Then send it to an agent. My sister is a literary agent, and she's helped a lot of new writers get started."

When I returned home to Longmeadow, I wrote to the agent in New York, and waited anxiously for an answer. It would be so important to work with someone who could guide me in the creating of a book. But good agents were hard to find and I'd heard that, as a rule, they took on only writers with great talent. It had been sweet of that lady to give me the name and address, but sisters very often are prejudiced.

However, a letter arrived promptly from the agent, saying she would be glad to see one or more of my stories. I mailed her one chapter of my manuscript and it seemed as though it had hardly had time to reach its destination before I received another letter. The agent liked the characters in my story and she thought it had possibilities. She had submitted it to a magazine editor who thought it read like one of a series. If I could write fifteen or sixteen Mama and Papa stories, the agent would work with me in the necessary rewriting and polishing. Of course she could make no promises, but she thought a book like the one I had begun would have an appeal to certain publishers.

I was dancing on air! My happiness knew no bounds. It seemed that God was directing this book. Everything was falling into its proper place! I knew I would succeed. There was no doubt in my mind that I would see my dream fulfilled and to have an enthusiastic agent take me under her wing was a great boost to my morale.

I had always written in longhand and typing had never entered my thoughts, but now I knew that I had to have a typewriter. So I took a bus to downtown Springfield and entered the largest stationery store to shop for one.

"Is it for your own use?" the clerk asked me.

My heart was beating rapidly and I gave him a mysterious look.

"Oh, yes," I answered, "it is for me. I'm an author and I must type my first book."

"Well, why don't you sit down and try this one?" he suggested.

I stared at him. "But I can't type! I've never had a typewriter before."

"Perhaps you should take lessons first."

"Oh, no, I don't have time for that. I'll learn quickly." I sat down and happily touched the white keys. "How much is it?" I asked.

He told me.

"I'll take this one."

The clerk looked pleased. "It's a good choice; a Smith-Corona is a good machine. Are you sure you want a portable?"

"Yes, that's best. Sometimes I'll want to move it around."

"Where shall I send it?" asked the clerk.

I looked tenderly at my shiny new typewriter. Suddenly I couldn't wait to get started.

"I'll take it," I decided.

The clerk looked at me in a strange way. He opened his mouth to speak, but evidently he changed his mind, for no words came out.

I stood beside him as he wrapped the machine in heavy paper, letting the handle stick out on the top so I could easily carry it. To me it was not the least bit heavy, and the bus was only a few feet from the store. I made my way home, walking the half-mile from the bus to our house. A song was in my heart. I felt heavy with words that kept piling up in my brain and longed to be placed on paper.

In front of a big window in our bedroom the card table was waiting. It looked just right with the new typewriter on it and the chair in front of it. I picked up a sheet of paper from a newly opened box and slid it into the machine; and then I sat down on the chair. With two fingers I typed my first words, the title of my book: *Papa's Wife*.

It was a big job, picking away with two fingers, but I had no idea that it would take five years from the time I began until the story was completed, that very often my back would ache and my fingers would be sore, that my chapters would go back and forth between my agent and me until she was pleased with my work. Only then could I begin a new chapter. But they were happy years, perhaps the happiest of my life. I had never realized how much time my writing would take up or how much I would enjoy it. Until then it had been only a dream in my heart, but now it was taking form and shape. I was thinking of the unknown years ahead of me. Mysteriously and challengingly they stretched into the future.

In those years I had to learn what discipline was. I was a wife and mother and housekeeper. My home and family were very important to me. I liked order and cleanliness, and I adored cooking; but now they all seemed to compete with my writing. Yes, there was laundry to do, and shopping, housecleaning, and entertaining. There were problems to talk over with the girls, and then there was the garden that my hands had always tended so anxiously. Now I found all those demands at war with each other. There was a great conflict between duty and this new love of sitting at the typewriter, creating from memory the happy story about my family. There were times when I wrote long into the night, and others when I would wake up from a sound sleep. I would sit up in bed with thoughts which came with such lucidity that I knew I had to get them down right then and there because in the morning they would be gone. On nights like this I blessed the portable, as I left my bed, slipped into my robe, picked up the typewriter, and went downstairs to the breakfast room.

Sometimes my husband would awaken, and hear the clicking keys in the distance. He would be very annoyed and scold me most severely.

"I've never objected to your writing in the daytime, but this night stuff I don't approve of at all. You've gone completely overboard since you got that agent. From now on I don't want to hear that typewriter at night again, and I mean it."

I obeyed his wishes, but my heart ached. Sometimes the finest and best ideas would pop into my head in the middle of the night. But how could I explain that to my Bob? He had not yet realized that writing was not a chore to me, and that I would go on with it whether or not my book was published. It had become a way of life for me, something that filled my whole being. It was a rhythm in my heart that had found an echo in the outside world. To be a whole person I had to play this game. Bob had never seen this side of me before in all the years I had been his wife. This was a mate he did not know. At times I must have seemed a stranger to my own husband, and perhaps it wasn't fair.

But it was strange and wonderful, this new world I had moved into, and life had never seemed so exciting to me before. It had a new meaning and I saw it in a different light, a light divided into small sections of glittering color calling and beckoning me.

I was still in that state of mind on New Year's Day, 1954, when the book was finished. I could not wait to send it off to my agent, who would present it to a publisher. I hoped that she would send it to the largest publishing company in America. I wanted to start at the top. I knew my book was good and different from other books. I felt that any publisher would be delighted to handle it. There was not a doubt in my mind that day that it would be accepted.

I looked for the last time at the big bundle of typewritten pages. I placed them in a box, wrapped it in brown paper, and tied it securely with heavy white string. My agent's address was clearly printed on it.

"Bob, will you drive me down to the American Express office?" I asked my husband. "I am sending my manuscript to the agent."

"Does it have to go today?" he inquired patiently.

"Yes, I want it to go right off. It's been so long in the making."

"Why don't you take the car yourself? You know how to drive."

I smiled and said, "Bob, this might seem silly to you, but I would like so very much just to sit and hold it until I have to part with it."

My husband drove me down to the American Express, and parked near the building.

"Any instructions for mailing it?" he asked, reaching for the box.

I clung to it. "I'll take it in," I said.

I presented the box to the man inside at the desk and he tossed it onto the scale. My heart almost broke. I wanted to ask him to be a little careful with it. After all, this was part of my heart; a dream was in that box. But he looked so cross that I just paid him the $2.38 and left the office.

Bob must have understood that this was not the time to talk. We drove home in silence to the strangeness of an empty typewriter and prepared for the long wait ahead.

❧ 3

I was never very good at waiting. In fact, having to wait for anything had always been one of the hardest things in life for me to bear. And now, because I could not face waiting for perhaps as long as a month to hear the fate of my manuscript, I had to keep my mind occupied in a very special way. Of course, there was no doubt that the publisher would accept the manuscript, and day after day this thought grew more and more positive. Faith is a thing not seen but hoped for. But my faith had to see, so already I visualized success. It would only be a little while, I reasoned, and what would prove my faith in a stronger way than to take a vacation at this time and spend the money I had not yet received? I could borrow from the household money and pay it back to Bob when I received a check from the publisher.

The girls were old enough to take care of their father and the household duties, so I decided to visit Mama in Miami, Florida, while I waited. Nothing could be more exciting, yet relaxing.

So one day in January, 1954, I boarded a train for Miami. I planned to stay a whole month. That, I figured, would give the publisher time to make up his mind; and when I returned from vacation, I would stop in New York City to receive the happy news and pick up my check. Then one day, at just the right time, I would ever-so-slightly wave the check under my husband's nose, and I would say, "Darling, when you married me, you had no idea you were marrying into money, did you?"

In Miami I had a wonderful time. There the sun was shining from a cloudless sky; at home there was snow and ice and cold. Each day Mama and I went to beautiful Miami Beach to lie on the golden sand and swim in the clear blue ocean. There were parties and barbecues in my doctor brother's yard and dips in his pool. We took trips to Key West and there were picnics and so much fun that the days which might have passed so slowly at home just flew by with lightning speed.

Every morning when I awoke, I would think about my book. I had pinned up little notes everywhere in my room where my eye could catch sight of them quickly. The notes consisted of two words: *Papa's Wife*. If positive thinking could produce results, I certainly did enough of it that month.

When I said good-bye to Mama and the rest of the family, I was still as sure as before that there would be no obstacles to the publication of my book. It would come through with flying colors! I waved and smiled, and my loved ones waved back. It had been wonderful being with Mama, and she too was excited about the book. After all, wasn't she its main character?

That night in a sleeper on the train I had a strange dream. It was the second time a dream had interfered with my happiness over the book. This time I was on the great ocean. I was all alone, drifting in a small boat. I had no idea where I was going or why I was there, yet the dream was very clear. A big wave came and washed me overboard; it carried me for miles until I was tossed up on a tiny island in the middle of nowhere. There were no people on the island, no trees, no signs of life—just hot brown sand. The sun was scorching me unmercifully and there was no help in sight. Then I awoke, delighted to find myself in a comfortable bunk on the train. But there was a dreadful feeling within me that I seemed unable to shake off. I sat up in my bunk and stared out into the night. This dream had a meaning. Had it been a warning? Perhaps all was not well with the manuscript. Perhaps the news would not be as good as I had expected. I tried to laugh it off but I couldn't go back to sleep. If only the night would pass. I would feel better in the morning, I told myself.

Morning finally came. When I stepped off the train in Pennsylvania Station, I rushed to a phone booth. I found the publisher's number in the Manhattan directory and dialed it quickly. I had to make sure of something. How fortunate I was to reach the editor in charge of my manuscript immediately. After exchanging greetings, I went right to the point.

"I'm calling about my manuscript," I said cheerfully. "I hope you have news for me."

It was quiet on the other end of the line for a moment, and then the editor responded. "Mrs. Bjorn, have you spoken to your agent?"

"Not yet," I answered lightheartedly, "I wanted to hear the good news directly from you, even if it isn't customary."

"I'm sorry," the editor said. "I dislike doing this. But since you have called, I have no other choice but to tell you—we did not take your manuscript."

"You did not take it!" The floor in the phone booth seemed to give way under my feet. "But why? Why?" I stammered. "It's a good book."

"I know it's a good book, a very good book, and we considered it for a time, but it doesn't fit into our present schedule."

There was no use talking. I understood that a decision had been made, and no words of mine could alter it. I had been a fool! I had broken the unwritten law that governs agent and writer. I had overstepped because of my lack of patience. Now I would have to face an angry agent as well as my disappointment and that would not be easy.

My agent was displeased, but I was contrite and apologetic; perhaps my foolish tears helped a little too. Perhaps she thought I had meted out my own punishment. After the tears had been dried, I blurted out my fears.

"But what will we do now? What will become of the book?"

My agent laughed and assured me that there were hundreds of publishers. The manuscript would be sent out again. . . .

Five words were still ringing in my ears when I arrived home: ". . . there are hundreds of publishers . . ." Someday one would take it. Someday—whenever that would be. Meanwhile, I was minus the money I had borrowed from our household account for my vacation. I had spent it on faith, but faith had failed me and there was no way for me to replace it. Bob was very nice about the whole thing. I'm sure he felt sorry for me, seeing the glow of my faith burned out. His words made me appreciate more than ever the man I had married.

"I was afraid this would happen, dear. You aimed too high. You seem to think that all you have to do is to believe in a thing to make it happen. I assure you, it isn't that easy. Perhaps your manuscript will never become a book with your name on it, but I'm proud of you just the same."

Then the tears had come again, but he wiped them away with his big handkerchief and I forced a smile to please him. It was good to be back home and I was relieved that the suspense was over. Most of all, it was good to have a husband who loved me whether or not I became an author. He was my security, a rock for me to lean on.

That was February, 1954. I knew it would take time to send the manuscript around to other publishers. I had to learn patience no matter how hard it was.

Then one day I made a great decision. I was not going to ask about the manuscript any more. I would just try to forget that I had written a book and leave the worrying about it to my agent. This would be hard to do, but I had to learn to have faith and patience. So I threw myself into household chores. I baked and cooked and entertained. I mingled with people and laughed and acted gay even though I was anxious. I never let on that there was the slightest doubt about eventual success. Perhaps it would have been better if I had not talked about the book, but I never succeeded in that one thing. You could just as easily have shut off Niagara Falls as shut me up. I had to talk about the book.

I might be riding on an airplane or bus with a perfect stranger beside me. We would smile at each other and as suddenly as lightning, out of a clear sky it would come.

"I have written a book!" That was how the words came. "Right now it's with a publisher in New York."

I would see the stranger's eyes open wide. "Oh, my, how interesting! I didn't realize I was sitting beside a celebrity. When is it coming out?"

I would smile a mysterious smile.

"It takes a little while to be accepted," I'd confide and then I'd relate parts of the story from my unpublished book. Luckily I was, by nature, a good storyteller and when the stranger and I parted, there was a notation in my purse for a notice to be sent to her address as soon as the book was on the market. Day by day the list grew until by the end of that summer I had eight hundred and five names of people interested in a manuscript that was still floating around New York, from publisher to publisher, where new readers were taking up the task of reading my story. I kept the list of names in a small red-velvet box tied with a wide ribbon. Every so often I would open it and read them, blessing each trusting person, sending a prayer up to God that I would never have to disappoint them.

Strangely enough I did live through that summer

even though no happy news reached me from my agent. At home we never mentioned the book any more. It was a closed issue. Even my daughters seemed to understand that their mother had suffered a heavy blow. I know the family wished that I had never attempted to write a book, but had just remained a mother and wife and housekeeper as I had been before.

It was that summer that I began to lecture for the Redpath Speaking Bureau. I almost shiver now as I think of how I dared to take on an assignment with such a dignified old speaking bureau, the oldest of its kind in America, I've been told. But my self-confidence never failed me. If I was tempted at times to be scared, I tried to remember that they had asked me after one of their representatives heard me tell a story to a storm-bound crowd at a religious gathering. So why should I worry? For some strange reason, they liked my style and had only required one thing from me—that I would never change, that I would always be myself—and that wasn't hard because it was the only way I knew how to be. I am grateful to Redpath for giving me such a fine start on my lecturing career.

My first engagement was in October. I was to speak before a woman's club on my unpublished book, on "How Mama Got Papa." I traveled two hundred miles that day. The club outdid itself in kindness and graciousness extended to me, and was very interested in the book.

"When is it coming out?" I was asked over and over again, and how it hurt every time I had to say that I didn't know; it still had not been accepted. But other clubs added more names to those already in the red box. No wonder I was anxious to hear the good news my agent had promised me would someday come.

Month after month passed and as December approached, I began to get discouraged for the first time. I fought off the deep depression that wanted to settle in my heart. I had learned from Mama that, when things look darkest, one must not give up, for just around the corner might hide success. I couldn't let all those people down. There had to be a book. And at last something happened during that summer that gave me new hope.

As usual I had gone to a retreat at Lake Winnipesaukee where I shared my worries about the manuscript with some wonderful people in a creative writing group. It was there that a sweet little lady had stood up and smiled at me.

"As you were speaking," she said, "the name of a publisher kept coming to my mind over and over again. I suggest that you send your manuscript to Rinehart and Company in New York City."

When I came home, I called my agent, telling her that it was important that I give her a message because again I had a strange feeling that God was directing the course of my book.

I was assured that Rinehart was one of the firms to which the manuscript was to be sent. The name had been on the list of prospective publishers right along.

Then my heart felt so light and I had so much faith. But months passed. Would this publisher reject it as others had done? There was no word from New York, and when Christmas arrived, I had given up hope. But I was not going to live the rest of my life with an unpublished book.

I would give each of my daughters one copy. It would become a type of family heirloom, passed down from generation to generation; and one day a young girl would hold up a brittle yellow manuscript and say, "My great great grandmother wrote this back in the 1950's." My work would not be entirely lost and that would have to satisfy my disappointed soul.

But then came December 30, 1954, and that day proved beyond the shadow of a doubt that nothing can destroy Faith when it is deeply rooted within the soul. I had a publisher! And that night of nights would never be forgotten. A new author was stepping into her rightful world with a script that had found favor in the sight

28

of the publishers—and a happier author had never lived. The future waited with its challenge. It was wonderful, more wonderful than words can tell.

❦4

"My life will never be the same," was the refrain that had been singing through my brain ever since *Papa's Wife* had been accepted, but I never could have dreamed how quickly it would change after a local paper revealed the news that a so-far-unknown Longmeadow housewife had written a book soon to be published.

How surprised I was at the number of telephone calls and letters which flooded in, congratulating me and making predictions about my future. But all of them wished me success. Students came from schools and colleges to ask me questions and, in addition to the Redpath Bureau's bookings, there were many speaking engagements at which I was to lecture on what had recently happened to me. My life became so busy I didn't know where to turn. Each new day I understood a little better what it meant to be in the public eye, that it was not an easy life, and that little by little you stopped functioning as yourself. At times I longed to go back to the uncomplicated person I had been when life had floated along like a stream and each day was dedicated just to my family. There were many lessons to learn during those first months of my new life.

One morning something very strange happened to me. It was late in March, on a cold, drizzly day with a wind blowing from the north. Something had gone wrong with our furnace and the house was completely without heat. While I waited for the repairman, who had assured me he would arrive before noon, I put on an old bathrobe of Bob's. It was a red woolen robe with a few moth holes in it. It was old and I had discarded it many times, but I loved to wrap up in it whenever I was cold, even if I had to fish it out of the Good Will bag. I promised myself each time that this was the very last time I would do something like this, but I always failed to keep those promises and up came the robe. That morning I had put cold cream on my face and rolled my hair up in curlers. I was not a pretty picture to behold, but I was comfortable in spite of the lack of heat.

It was exactly 8:23 A.M. when the front doorbell chimed. Thinking it was the paper boy who did not want to leave the newspaper out in the rain, I hurried to open the door. But there, outside in the drizzly rain, stood a man. He was an old man, small in stature, but erect, with a round face and blue eyes that twinkled as he spoke. On his head was a round cap with a brim. When I opened the door, he smiled a wide smile.

"Excuse this early morning hour," he said, "but I was walking by and I've recently read in the newspaper that an author lives in this house. I've never seen a real live author. Could I make an appointment to meet her?"

Then when he saw my embarrassment, he misunderstood it and continued rapidly: "Oh, I have nothing really to say to her. All I want is just to look . . . just to see her. Is that too much to ask?"

"Not at all," I said, drawing Bob's bathrobe closer around my body. "Mister, you are looking at her right now!"

His eyes grew a little larger, but his gaze never left my face. For a few seconds we stared at each other; then he turned away without even a word of farewell.

31

I stood there in the doorway and watched him walk away. If only he had said something more, perhaps that bad taste would not be in my mouth. I had been too honest. I had hurt and disappointed him. Perhaps it would have been kinder to have made an appointment with him for later that day and to have had him meet me as I sat by my typewriter or some other object that would have provided a proper setting for an author. But it had happened so suddenly that I had been taken off guard, and being me, I had not thought of scheming. But it was done now and surely he would never meet another author in exactly the same way. I can still see him in my mind's eye as I think back—turning around, walking up the hill and disappearing, the small round head on that small body, the brimmed cap and the eyes that twinkled when he spoke. But even if I had let the man down, I had learned a new lesson.

And the red robe went into the Good Will bag for keeps, and I would never have the comfort of it again. It seemed the only way I could square myself with the little man who wanted so badly to see a real live author.

So often now I wish that I could always retain the feeling of those first few months—the bubbling over within me, the zest and joy of living, the fun of being me. The whole world had a silver lining and the melody of happiness seemed to be playing everywhere. God had never seemed closer to me. I awoke each new morning with a feeling of anticipation, wondering what this day would bring, and each was full to the brim and running over with new events.

One day that same spring there came a letter from Philadelphia, Pennsylvania, as the result of a clipping from the Springfield newspaper containing an interview in which I had referred to the Swedish-Finnish author, Fredrika Bremer, as my childhood ideal, who had inspired me to begin to write. I was now informed that a Fredrika Bremer Committee was part of the American-Swedish Museum in Philadelphia. Would I honor them with my membership? There was also an invitation to travel to Sweden the following summer with a few selected women who had contributed in some way toward bringing America and Sweden closer together. We were to carry greetings from our adopted land and to try to interest the Swedish women in our museum.

It was such a special letter and its contents were so thrilling that I accepted with pleasure. I was very naïve, taking the invitation literally, and it wasn't until later that I was told the cost of such a trip and that I was to pay my own fare. That, of course, changed the picture for a while until my family decided that I should take the opportunity, especially because of the many exciting things that were included in the trip's agenda. The most important event to me was the visit we had been granted with her Majesty, the Queen of Sweden, to bring her greetings from the American-Swedish museum she had visited as a crown princess many years ago when the cornerstone had been laid. It was not often that an invitation was given to visit a queen, and I looked forward to the summer of 1956 when all this would take place. Part of the first check I would receive from the publisher would go for this trip.

I was a lucky person to have all this come to me. Already a special copy of *Papa's Wife,* bound in moroccan leather trimmed in gold, was in the making. I was to present it to her as a gift.

Soon after I had agreed to join the group on the trip to Sweden, another invitation came for me to give a lecture in the American-Swedish museum on a Sunday afternoon for a very select group of Scandinavians. They wanted me to speak about the book.

By this time it was on the market, and seeing it in print and on display in bookstores everywhere made me feel very humble and grateful. It was such a beautiful book and the artist who had designed the jacket had done a magnificent job. I felt like a real author. I had autographed hundreds of books in bookstores and for people who called at my home after they had bought a copy. Memories of the autographing parties, which had been so successful, still lingered in my heart.

It was a beautiful day when I arrived in Philadelphia. My sister Margaret, who lived there, met me and took me to her cute apartment to relax before my speech. There were to be many special guests at the museum that afternoon. Perhaps the most prominent one was Madam Kronvall, the wife of the Swedish consul to the United States. She was such a gracious, charming person. A dinner was given for us at one of the large hotels before we gathered with the rest of the people at the beautiful museum.

The auditorium was packed and we were given a royal welcome. Swedish songs were sung by famous singers. Madam Kronvall presented the museum with a large Swedish flag, which was placed at the front of the auditorium.

That flag did something to me. I had not seen such a large flag of my native land since 1935 when I had last visited Sweden, and many memories began to storm upon me. In my mind I was a little girl again, running up the Swedish hills and mountains, seeing everywhere the flag that had once been mine. It was not mine any more. I had given it up when I became an American citizen, and The Star-Spangled Banner had taken its place. I loved my new country and I took pride in its flag, but I was only its adopted child. Now at this gathering, the old motherland spoke to me through the flag that stood there so gloriously with its gold cross on the heavenly blue. It was a beautiful flag which made my heart beat fast and brought a lump to my throat.

Then the lady who was to introduce me began to speak. And to my surprise, I recognized her as the daughter of another Swedish minister from the city where my Papa had served as pastor. She was my age, or perhaps a little younger, and she began her introduction by telling a story:

"Many years ago," she said, "on a beautiful summer day, my sisters and brother and I were walking with my preacher father in a lovely park in our home town. Suddenly our attention was drawn to the chatter of happy voices coming up one of the paths in the park. A middle-aged man with gray hair and a cap on his head, was leading at least six children up the walk and all of them seemed to be talking at once. And they were talking in Swedish . . ."

As she spoke, I was back there, one of those children, laughing and talking as Papa showed us the park of that city to which we had come from Sweden only three days before. Suddenly I wished that I could live those years over again, that I could see and talk to Papa once more, and the lump in my throat grew twice as large as before and tears formed beneath my eyelids, but I had to hold them back. The lady was almost through with her introductory speech.

"And now," she said, "it gives me the greatest pleasure to introduce to you one of those children I saw in the park that day so many years ago—a girl who grew up to become an author and also one of the most humorous speakers you will ever hear. . . ."

She mentioned my name, the people applauded, and I mounted the platform. But the lump in my throat would not go away. I tried to smile, but the smile would not come. The clapping stopped. I took off my glasses and placed them on the lectern, and I dabbed at my eyes with my handkerchief.

"Thank you," I said softly. "Thank you, Madam Kronvall, for letting me look at the beautiful Swedish flag; and thank you, my friend from so many years back in time when we both walked with our papas. Thank you all for the warm welcome you have given me. But I must confess I can't talk, not now, not yet. I can't talk because I have to cry."

And the tears came as I was unable to hold them back any longer. They rolled down my cheeks and I tried to wipe them away as fast as they came. But it seemed there was no end to them. They just wouldn't stop.

Then as I looked out over the people, some of them began to cry too. Sophisticated ladies dabbed their eyes with their lace handkerchiefs; others cried unashamedly; men blew their noses hard and up came their big white handkerchiefs until wherever I looked I saw dabs of white all over the auditorium and nearly five hundred people crying. Perhaps, like me, they had memories. Perhaps they remembered their papas. Perhaps some cried just to keep the rest company. I had never seen anything like it. It was really funny.

Suddenly, instead of crying, I wanted to laugh at the whole thing. So I wiped my eyes for the last time, put on my glasses, and smiled at the people.

"And now," I said, "I'm going to give you the funniest talk I have ever given."

And I think I did because people were soon laughing so hard they nearly fell off their chairs, and some of them cried and laughed at the same time. I felt so free and relieved. I don't think I have ever enjoyed making a speech quite as much as I did that afternoon in Philadelphia.

At the reception that evening I talked with people for hours it seemed. Perhaps those people had needed to cry that afternoon, just as I did, to make room for the laughter and fun that was to come later and make us all feel happy and free. I know they never held the crying against me.

They were dear people. We were all adopted children in a great new land, and we knew that this motherland, like the old one, would never let us down. So we were rich, being able to claim two great heritages. And I was the most blessed of all to be able to bring both tears and laughter to so many people.

ᘉ5

It is always fun getting ready for a trip to the old country, and this was a very special one because it was especially designed to give us a wonderful time and an opportunity to visit many prominent people. There would also be time for me to visit with my own relatives and to take a few side trips to England, Holland, and Denmark. These countries had also published my book, and I had a longing to walk among their people and be a small part of them, even if I could spend only a day or two in each country.

The glow of becoming an author still warmed my heart. I couldn't get over the wonder of it all or the knowledge that my book had climbed onto the bestseller list in both the New York *Times* and the New York *Herald Tribune* and was selling extremely well all over the country. Mail poured in from people who loved it, and I was kept busy answering letters and telephone calls from people previously unknown to me. It seemed there were no problems in the world except one, and that one seemed to grow in size with each new day. It even began to overshadow the glow of my lovely trip, which, for a little while, had to be placed in the background as I struggled to find a fair solution.

I had made up my mind from the very beginning

that authorship must never interfere with my family life. I had not written a book to be famous or to make money or to become better than the rest of my own people. I had done it because writing was a natural instinct, a natural mode of expression, and had been for as long as I could remember. The joy of creating filled me and that was what had inspired the words which made my book a success.

I knew my husband and girls were proud of me, but still there was a little something that worried me. Bob made little remarks every now and then about his wife becoming independent—saying now I could buy what I wanted, so why discuss purchases with him when I had my own income. It hurt me every time he said something like that. Bob had been a wonderful husband, and he had worked hard all his life to give his family many luxuries which some with larger incomes lacked. I had my own checking account into which he put a certain sum each week. I had my own car and I seldom felt that I needed to ask him about buying things because he always said, "That's your department, dear. If you can afford it, go ahead." We had always had wonderful vacations in the summertime. Bob usually sent the girls and me to a cottage in the mountains or at Cape Cod and he joined us during his vacation. I had charge accounts, and I loved to use them. If I didn't have enough, Bob always filled in. There were times when I overstepped my bounds and he should have put his foot down; he always planned to, but when it came right down to it, he usually let the incident slip by.

I remember standing, one cold winter day long ago, outside a furrier's window, peering in at the coats displayed on dummies. There was one coat that took my fancy. It was a brown, Alaskan sealskin—the most beautiful thing I had ever seen. Like a sleepwalker I was drawn into the store and asked about it. At the time the price seemed enormous. It was almost one thousand dollars. But I tried it on, since the clerk was nice enough to take it off the dummy and bring it to me. It was the only one of its kind in that particular style. It fitted me like a glove, and, oh, did I feel like someone special in that coat!

"I'll take it," I said, knowing we had an installment account there. "I'd like to pay fifteen dollars down on it."

The clerk was very obliging, and I left the shop with the coat in a big box under my arm, more thrilled than if I had had a million dollars in my pocket.

When I reached home, I called Bob.

"Dear," I said jubilantly, "I bought the most wonderful thing downtown today. You'll never guess what it is in a million years!"

"What is it?" he teased. "A new hat?"

"No, it's much bigger than that and it cost a little bit more. Oh, you'll just love it! I bought an Alaskan sealskin coat!"

"You did what?" came the voice from the other end.

"I bought a coat," I went on. "It's beautiful. It was just made for me!"

"What did it cost?"

"I only paid fifteen dollars down," I replied.

"What was the full price?"

"Not quite a thousand dollars."

There was quiet on the other end of the line for a long, long time. Then finally my husband's voice came sharp and demanding.

"What makes you think you can go around buying fur coats for a thousand dollars? You're no child. You should know better. You put that coat in its box and take it back this afternoon, and tell them *I* said you had to."

But I didn't take it back. I just couldn't. It was as if it had been made especially for me. I wanted that fur coat more than I wanted any other article of clothing. I didn't say anything more about it, but I hung it in my closet. Many times during the day when Bob was at work I tried it on. Several times I put it on and wore it walking up and down the street. Then one day, when we were going out with friends to a dinner party, I wore it, I realized that my husband was very quiet that evening, but he did not speak to me about the coat. He paid for it little by little, and I wore it for at least fifteen years. Then it was remodeled into a lovely, useful jacket. Now, after at least twenty-five years, one of my daughters has had it made over into a cute little evening jacket. Poor Bob! How childish I was. But it was a fine coat and we certainly saved in the long run on the many others I would have had to have during those years. So it was not a bad investment after all.

I remembered how good Bob had been about all those things, and now when I was to have my own money coming twice a year from the publisher, he must not be hurt because of it. He had been too wonderful and kind to me during our married years. As I was trying to find a way to handle this so that life could go on the way it had before, the problem solved itself.

At that time we lived in an old, two-story house in Longmeadow, from which we had a glorious view of the sunset. But the house was too formal and had too many stairs and I never felt that my roots could be planted deep enough to take hold there.

One day a friend called me and asked if I wanted to go with her to look at a lovely new ranch-style house which was for sale in an attractive part of our town.

"I had planned to buy it," she told me, "but the deal is off because my husband and I simply cannot come to any agreement about it. He's just not ready to buy a new house right now, but I want to take one last look at it. It's such a nice house and exactly what I've always wanted."

I agreed to go, so she picked me up in her car and we drove to the address. It was a wonderful house, and when I first stepped into it, I felt as if I had always lived there. Just as with the fur coat so long ago, I knew this was my house—it belonged to me. While my friend was talking to the salesman, I wandered about in the rooms, aware of a quiet, homey welcome.

"This is my house," I said to myself. "I love it."

The sun was pouring its gold through the bright, shiny windows making it a garden of sunshine. I looked out toward the sky and I spoke to God. "I'd like to have this house!" I said.

Then came the same soundless voice I had known when I had talked to God about becoming an author many years before: "If you like it that much, you can have it."

I spoke out loud, "Do you mean it? Really?"

I could feel the answer. It was affirmative . . . and the house was mine from that moment on. I asked my husband to look at it at noon. He did and he liked it, too. Wasn't it too bad we were in no position to buy it?

"It will be my project," I told him. "I want life to go on for us just as it always has. You give me my weekly budget money and what I earn lecturing and writing will go toward this house until it is paid for."

He thought that was a good idea, and at six o'clock that night I saw the real-estate man and I made a fifty-dollar deposit. The rest of the down payment was to come from the sale of our old house and a thousand from my royalty check, which I expected at the end of April.

That is the way we have worked the nine years that we have lived here. I am as dependent upon my husband as before, but in a way he is also dependent upon me, which makes a very good family combination, and our money is always put in the proper place. I was free to carpet the house, buy shrubbery and furniture, and Bob never interfered as long as I could pay for it. He made the monthly payments and I reduced the principal each year in a sizable way. This was a good way to solve the money problem and still keep me dependent, as I think a woman should be to fill her rightful place in life and to be happy with her man.

What a busy time we had moving into a brand-new house. Wonders never ceased. The old house sold quickly; within two weeks we had a buyer. God was good to us to let it happen so soon, for in another couple of weeks I would be leaving with the Fredrika Bremer Committee to take that wonderful trip to my homeland, not just as a visitor, but to represent America in a special way, to meet all kinds of new people, and to be a guest in prominent homes—all experiences my wildest girlhood dreams could never have anticipated. It was hard to sleep nights with my lovely new bedroom filled with suitcases, and clothes and more clothes everywhere—special dresses for special occasions.

Then came the day when Bob and my younger daughter, Carolyn, drove me to New York to the airport where I met the other ladies. It was fun to go, but still, as I waved good-bye to my loved ones, I couldn't help wishing that I was back again in my new home and in my new world in which I had lived such a short time.

❧ 6

The huge airplane lifted and soon we were flying high up among the white clouds. I leaned back in the comfortable seat and relaxed. How I had waited for this event to take place, counting the days until my flight home. Yes, I called it home, although I had been living in America for so many years. But sitting there in that plane I still felt as though I belonged to Sweden. Perhaps, I was thinking, the land in which you are born demands your first love.

As a child I had possessed a passionate love for my country. It was the year 1924; my family and I had left Sweden and moved to the United States. What a blow it had been to my young heart when word had come so suddenly that Papa had accepted a new pastorate, a Swedish church in far-off America. until then I had been happy and carefree among my mountains and lakes and the waterfalls and valleys. I had walked familiar paths in the dark green forest unaware of how quickly one's destiny could change. Leaving for a new world had made my blood tingle with excitement, but only those who have left a native land can understand the emotions that tear the heart as well. How many beautiful dreams had been mine in the endless white summer nights of my Sweden. Those dreams had come true in my adopted land.

As that night passed slowly, I knew each moment brought us nearer and nearer our destination. Four small jubilant words kept singing in my ears: "I am going home." Like a bird I was winging myself over the endless waters.

This journey would widen our horizon and strengthen the tie between Sweden and America. That was the aim of the American-Swedish Historical Foundation and its museum, which we represented, and all of us would try to do our best in every little detail to fulfill this great obligation we had undertaken.

Morning arrived! There was a misty rose sky into which the sun stepped from his chamber, and there below us were the tiny lakes, the dark forests, dotted with red and white homes and green, green meadows. It was Sweden—Sweden in her morning glory, welcoming her daughters home.

The landing was smooth and beautiful and as I stepped out of the plane onto Swedish soil, despite the happiness in my heart there was a lump in my throat and my eyes filled with tears. For a second I had a wild desire to be dramatic, to throw myself on the ground and kiss it. But the emotion passed as quickly as it had come and I felt calm once more, fascinated by the warm welcome we received. I had never before been a part of a group that had been met by a delegation with a band playing, bouquets of flowers for everyone, and speeches in pure, unmixed Swedish. Two automobiles with drivers were designated as ours during our stay in Gothenburg, the great seaport city where we had landed, and of course the press was there with photographers. I began to understand how very important our mission was, though I had known from the start that I was going to enjoy it. It would be wonderful to be spoiled and pampered for a while and I felt as though I had moved into a fairy world where any wish would be granted.

The days that followed were indeed exciting—parties, luncheons, dinners, and teas in our honor; and sight-seeing trips in boats, by car, and on foot. Parks,

44

museums, and elegant restaurants became daily routine. Everything seemed perfect when suddenly a cloud covered the sun and I was face to face with my greatest disappointment.

It came at the end of a wonderful day. The committee chairman called a meeting in her hotel room. We could tell by the look on her face that something was wrong.

"I have very disappointing news for you," she began. "I dread having to tell you that our visit with the Queen of Sweden was canceled this afternoon."

The room was deathly silent. In the tense stillness I was sure the others could hear my heart pounding. It was beating as though it would come out of my body. I must have heard incorrectly, I was thinking; it just couldn't be true.

But our chairman continued: "I had a telephone call from Stockholm this afternoon; the Queen's Lady-in-Waiting was most apologetic when she told me that there have been so many official and social functions that Queen Louise is all tired out and has to have some rest. So all appointments have been canceled and they are packing to leave for her summer palace in Skane. What could I do about it? There's nothing to do but take this graciously and know that at least we were on the royal agenda for a half a year."

Everyone seemed to accept this bravely—everyone but me.

It was largely because of the visit with the Queen of Sweden that I had decided to take this trip. It had promised to be such an exciting experience. As always, I had bubbled over and soon everyone had known about the royal visit. My publisher had agreed that I might order a very special copy of *Papa's Wife* to present to Her Majesty. It was a beautiful book and I had held it in my hands and rehearsed the words I would speak as I presented it. It was very exciting! The news had traveled around and one day a reporter from the daily newspaper had called with a camera and snapped my picture holding the book. It appeared on the front page with an article about my "approaching visit" with Queen Louise: "Longmeadow Author Will Soon Have an Audience with the Queen of Sweden." It had been a lovely write-up and the telephone had rung for days after that with many good people congratulating and advising me about visiting royalty. And I had promised the newspaper another story when I returned. How could I tell them there had been no visit! What in the world would I do? I couldn't keep my heartache to myself, so I burst out at our fine chairman who already carried too many burdens.

"If only you had hinted that there was a possibility that we would not see the Queen I would never have talked about it, and I surely would not have had my picture in the paper. What shall I tell them when I return without having had the visit?"

My outburst did not set very well with the chairman; in fact, she disliked every word I had said. I had taxed her patience to the limit. She glared angrily at me, and her words fell like hammer blows.

"We are all heartbroken about this," she snapped, "even if we didn't have our pictures in the newspaper. We all had our hopes and dreams. To get an audience with a queen is not easy. If you don't believe me, just try for yourself."

"I might just do that," I said meekly. "It might be the only way out. I have to see the Queen."

I'm sure no one paid the slightest attention to my words. The other ladies soon forgot the misfortune. It was a closed door and they accepted it graciously, as ladies should. But not me! I stormed inwardly. A closed door was something I had never accepted. If it did not open as expected, there had to be another way to get inside. An obstacle had always been a challenge to me. This was one which I must tackle and I knew it would take everything my brain could think up to accomplish it.

After discarding many ideas, I finally decided to write a letter to Her Majesty. I would step out on my own and not tell her I was a member of the Fredrika Bremer Committee.

Then I remembered a conversation I had had with Mama the last time she had visited me in Longmeadow. I had told her then about my trip to Sweden and my anticipation of seeing the Queen. Mama had laughed in her happy, carefree way and her eyes had twinkled as they always did when she was ready to spring something on us.

"I'm not so surprised about your visit with the Queen. It must run in the family."

"What do you mean, Mama?" I had asked in amazement.

"Oh, didn't I ever tell you about the time I presented the roses to the King of Sweden?"

"No, I never heard that! Did you really?"

"Yes. It was when I was a girl of fourteen and worked as a nursemaid for the Royal Gardener's little boy. There was to be a big parade one day. The King was to ride through the park on his fine horse, and the little boy was supposed to present His Majesty with a bouquet of red roses. But when the moment arrived and the King came galloping down the road, the little boy, who was only three, became very bashful and hid in my skirts and began to cry. Then one of the high officials suggested that the nursemaid present the roses. And I did. I made myself as tall and straight as I could and curtsied all the way to the ground. The King was so nice. He patted my cheek and smiled at me. Oh, that was one of the greatest moments of my life."

I was glad that Mama had told me her story because, as I wrote my letter, I was able to tell the Queen about it and then go on to relate how the nursemaid had married a minister and moved to America. Now her daughter had written a book about the mother, a very funny book, and I asked in my very best manner if I could visit Her Majesty and present her with a copy of the book—a copy which had been made especially in her honor. I made inquiry and saw that the letter was sent to the right person in order to reach the Queen.

My hopes were high again; I had a feeling that it was going to work.

One day our committee took a trip to a nearby province. Through the American Consulate, we had received permission to visit two cousins of America's first lady, Mamie Eisenhower. It was the first time I had realized that Mrs. Eisenhower was of Swedish descent. It was a lovely day and the Swedish countryside had never been more beautiful.

The Rudolf Larsons lived in a little dream house surrounded by a beautiful garden where all the flowers were in full bloom. They received us graciously; the coffee was ready and we enjoyed delicious pastries and many kinds of wonderful cookies. They were such perfect hosts and made us feel so welcome. They showed us pictures of Mamie as a little girl in America from the big family album. Mrs. Magda Franson joined the Larsons, and it was interesting to talk with these ladies related to our First Lady. Our talk was mostly of America and the White House.

It is a beautiful memory now, that lovely forenoon with those dear people. They were simple, kind, and warmhearted, and as we left, part of our hearts remained there. I was glad that our First Lady had such a wonderful background; it made me feel so much closer to her. We did share something precious in common.

The next day we left wonderful Gothenburg for Stockholm. Instead of taking the train, our chauffeur drove us through that beautiful section of Sweden. I was sitting in the front seat and it seemed to me that we were going very fast. I looked over at the speedometer as it registered eighty . . . eighty-five . . . ninety . . . ninety-five. The roads we traveled were narrow and I wondered how fast we were traveling in American miles. I new there was a free speed limit in Sweden, but for my comfort, we were moving much too fast.

Finally I asked the driver, "Please tell me how fast we are going in American miles."

"Lady," he said, "this car is a Buick, an American car, so the speed is indicated in American miles."

My heart almost stopped for a moment.

"You mean at times we drive ninety-five miles an hour!"

"I can go faster," he bragged.

The other ladies were as alarmed as I. It seemed I had spoken for all of us.

"We don't want to go that fast. If you don't slow down to fifty or sixty, we'd prefer to walk to Stockholm."

He slowed down immediately, but he looked dejected. "I wanted to please you by driving fast," he muttered. "Here people talk about how fast you drive in America. You come from there and you want me to slow down to fifty. . . . I can't understand it."

Poor man, he had to drive slowly to Stockholm and he was not at all happy with our attitude. But we arrived there safely and soon new festivities began. At a beautiful hotel on Saltsjöbaden, a few miles outside of the city, we took up our residence. It was a hot summer day, as hot as in America. We had very little time to relax as there was a luncheon being given in our honor by a lady belonging to the Swedish parliament.

While we were dressing for the luncheon, two of the committee members decided to speak only Swedish from that moment on. They wanted to learn the language and thought this a good way to start. It was fun for me, an expert in Swedish, to converse with them. But as we sat in the taxi going into Stockholm, I was very much surprised to have one of them tell me in Swedish: *"Du är talaren."* (You are the speaker.)

I was astonished! Here we were, driving to the luncheon, and only now was I told that I was supposed to speak. How could they give me so little notice? I knew my Swedish, but it certainly was not a thoughtful act to tell me half an hour before . . .

"You mean today?" I asked.

The other answered in Swedish, "I mean at this luncheon."

So, I gathered that I was to be the speaker on this important occasion. I had no subject other than my book, but I would tell about it as well as I could, tying in our two countries. I would do my best; it was all I could do.

What a beautiful dining room. What elegance! And the table—how can I ever forget the sight of it?—a long table, the length of the room, set for forty people. The snow-white cloth was decorated with small bunches of wild flowers and at intervals along the table were large, low vases of flowers. The exquisite china and heavy silver spoke of perfect taste; then suddenly my eyes focused on something else. At each place stood a number of small glasses, I can't remember exactly how many, all filled to the brim with wines and liquors, one kind for each course. I learned later that this was the only proper way of drinking in Sweden, but I had had no such experience in my parsonage home. This was a part of official social life, but not of mine. The liquids looked beautiful in the crystal glasses and it was a hot day. The Swedes do not serve water with their meals, not even coffee, and I was thirsty, very thirsty.

As we sat down, I wondered how strong the liquors were and if one kind was weaker than the others. As I was thinking, I fingered one glass; and presently a gentleman across the table from me got to his feet. He lifted his glass high and smiled at me broadly.

"Let us all drink a skoal to Fru Björn," he called out.

All the guests lifted their glasses and drank happily in my honor. I lifted my glass too, slowly and a bit uncertainly; I could feel Papa's eyes on me from the other world. Somehow the glass found my lips, although I tried not to get even a drop down. But I had to skoal with the rest, if that was what was required of me.

As the luncheon proceeded, the gentleman beside me

rose and lifted his glass, calling out the same words as the man before him.

"Let us drink a skoal to Fru Björn."

And they all drank happily again. This time some of the liquor went down my throat. I was bewildered and unhappy. If they wanted to drink, why did they all drink to me, who didn't drink? This happened a few more times, and I know now that it must have been because my fingers touched a glass. I learned later that a lady in Sweden never drinks at a meal unless a gentleman drinks to her. But if she is dying of thirst, she puts her finger on a glass and a gentleman obliges by drinking a skoal to her. How ashamed I was at my behavior, all because of my ignorance in those matters.

But that was only one of my troubles. I was to be the speaker, yet not one word had been said about it except those words in the taxi. I knew there must be some time at which I was supposed to give my talk. I tried to get the eye of our chairman and finally I succeeded. I talked with my eyes; she smiled back at me. I pointed to myself and she nodded. I took that as my cue and stood up, smiling at the people.

"I feel like sharing a funny story with you that began in Sweden and ended in America," I said, and the people applauded loudly, which gave me the needed courage. I began my lecture and there was much gaiety and laughter. I talked for almost an hour, and when I was through, we were rushed to our taxis. There was a tea being given in our honor by Countess Bernadotte; and if we did not leave immediately, we would be late. We only had a minute in which to thank our hostess and scramble into our cars to reach Drottningholm in time. It was to be a wonderful afternoon. The Countess had invited the American Woman's Club of Stockholm as special guests, and there would be more food and fun and laughter and many new charming people to meet. I rode in the taxi with our chairman.

"If it hadn't been for your long talk, we would have been on time," she said wearily.

"I'm sorry," I said, a bit hurt, "but no one told me how long to speak."

"No one told you to speak at all," she stormed.

I stared at her, hardly believing what I had heard.

"What do you mean?" I demanded.

"I mean just what I said. Whatever possessed you to get up and speak? The lecturer never had a chance to say one word."

"The lecturer?" I gasped.

"He was an old and refined gentleman, and a fine speaker, I'm sure."

I have never felt more foolish. Instead of going to another party, I wanted to go back to my hotel room and hide. I found out later that it was all a silly mistake occasioned by two ladies trying to speak only in Swedish. They had meant to say to me, *"Vem är talaren?"* (Who is the speaker?). Instead one had said,, *"Du är talaren."* (You are the speaker).

They were as upset about the incident as I was, and I forgave them. In spite of the mistake, it had been fun to share my story, and I had done it in good faith. My satisfaction was the memory of all the laughter. Even if I had taken someone else's place, I gave my victims a good time.

❧ 7

It was on a beautiful day in Stockholm that we drove to Årsta castle, a bit outside the city, to visit the home of Fredrika Bremer, for whom our committee was named.

I felt small and insignificant there, looking up at the massive stone structure where the author of my dreams had lived for so many years. It could very well have been a prison, I was thinking, and perhaps Fredrika often thought so too as her heart yearned for freedom. I was impressed with the largeness of the rooms, the magnificent paintings, the beautiful silver and crystal. There was also the old clock which played melancholy tunes. We were told by our guide that Fredrika's father, Mr. Bremer, often used to play this clock in the dead of night, trying to find relief from the torment of an evil spirit which often beset him.

To walk in those rooms was to feel that you knew Fredrika Bremer much better. How many tears she must have shed when her strict father made her sit and study day and night. It must have seemed to her that there would never be enough time to do the things her heart desired. How could she expand and reach out when enclosed within these walls? How could she outgrow the old and embrace the new?

I stood by the window beside her desk. Here it was that she wrote, and it was in this room that her spirit found release from her body. She had looked out over the same beautiful setting of fields, woodlands, and sky. I felt so close to her spirit in that room, but even closer when we made a pilgrimage to her grave.

There was a large, ancient stone church, cold and solemn as death itself—Österhannige church. Strangely enough a funeral was going on at that moment, which made the setting even more realistic. With reverence and awe we walked slowly on the stony paths toward the Bremer family grave under the big trees. We read the names on the old tombstone and placed our flowers on the grave with a silent greeting from the museum in Philadelphia—in America—where the Fredrika Bremer Room will always remind the world of this great woman. The custom in Sweden was that there should be a speech at the grave, and I was asked to give it. I know there were tears in my eyes and the words came from the depths of my heart.

"Fredrika Bremer, you are not dead. You are living in the hearts of all women who love freedom, and you will live on and on for freedom's sake and for the sake of right and of humanity."

As we left this sacred spot, there was a soft whisper in the swaying treetops, as though her spirit spoke to us, especially to me. She had long been my ideal and in my thoughts she walked beside me out through the gate into the world outside.

It was on a Sunday that we took a tour of Upsala City, renowned the world over for its university. There was the old and new Upsala. In the morning we worshiped in the historical state-church and then moved to Odenborg, an old inn, where we were entertained by a baron and baronness. There we drank ale called *mjöd* from an old ox-horn. We all took one sip of this mysterious light drink from the drinking horn which, of course, was lined with metal. Distinguished names were carved on it—names which now belong to history—of people who had put their lips to this same horn hundreds of years ago. *Queen Kristina, King Gustave Adolfus, King Karl the fourteenth, Johan,* and many, many more names were engraved in silver. How I loved these old things! These were what made Sweden so enchanting to me—its history that dates way back to the nine—eight—seven hundreds and even further back. If only I had learned more about it when I lived there.

There was so much to see, and as we walked into the old castles and historical places, our guide told us tales of love, tears, executions, blood baths, and terrible adventures of the Vikings. Yes, we walked on the hills where the old kings were buried, hills which have been there since Sweden was a heathen country. How strange and mysterious it all seemed!

It was a day well spent and I was tired but happy when I stepped into the lobby of my hotel in Saltsjöbaden. The clerk informed me that there had been several telephone calls for me during the day. I was to call back if I returned before ten o'clock that evening, but if it was later than that, they would call back at nine the next morning. The calls had come from Hälsingborg. I was puzzled. Who would call me from that city? I had no acquaintances there. Then slowly a thought came into my mind.

"Please tell me," I said. "Is Queen Louise's summer castle, Sofiero, in that vicinity?"

They informed me that it was.

"Then," I said with all the joybells ringing in my heart, "the call was from Her Majesty, the Queen."

The clerk took a second look at me, and I felt as if I had grown in importance. His eyes followed me as I walked to the elevator, perhaps wondering who I was to rate a phone call from the Queen of Sweden.

It was hard for me to go to sleep that night; I was too excited. Tomorrow I would know whether or not I could visit the Queen; and even if I could not, at least I could say she had been in touch with me.

I must have slept some during the night, but I awoke early. Too excited to eat breakfast, I wanted to order something, so I ordered a dish of prunes and some black coffee. When the busboy came with my order, there was a small dish of prunes, black coffee, and a large bowl of whipped cream. I had never eaten whipped cream for breakfast before, but I did that morning, feeling this could be called a breakfast fit for a queen. As I ate, I waited for the telephone to ring. And ring it did, exactly at nine o'clock.

There was a sweet voice on the other end, which identified itself as that of the Queen's Lady-in-Waiting. She had a message for me from Queen Louise. Her Majesty would love to have me visit her, and if it was convenient for me, the Queen would see me at her summer castle outside of Hälsingborg on July 3, at ten o'clock in the morning; and she sent her warmest greetings and bid me a hearty welcome.

Wasn't that wonderful? I don't think I had ever felt such a thrill. There were not too many days to wait until my heart's desire would be fulfilled.

Those days passed quickly. I took a trip to the northern part of Sweden to visit my relatives. The mission of the committee was over, and we were now all on our own. Then one day I stepped off the train in Hälsingborg, found a hotel, and prepared for the royal visit.

How does one dress when she has an audience with a queen? I had not asked. I wanted to be myself in every way, so I decided to dress simply. Since it was a hot July, I wore a white suit, with hat and shoes to match. I looked like myself and I knew I would act like myself, too, in spite of my excitement. It was hard to sleep that night. I did a lot of thinking, amazed at all the things which had happened to me since I was a little girl in Sweden, dreaming daring dreams which had become reality. But in my wildest dreams, I had never gone as far as thinking that one day I would be invited to a castle to see and speak to the Queen.

After breakfast that morning I called a taxi. In Sweden, as in America, taxis line up and wait their turn. There were all sorts of taxis, but when mine drove up to the door of the hotel, it looked to me as though it had come out of the ark. It was an old car and the front seat was a little higher than the back. When the driver spoke to me, I couldn't quite understand him because he spoke with a rural Skåne dialect, which is the hardest dialect to understand. I wanted to talk to him about things and places as we drove out into the country, so I asked if he minded if I rode in the front seat. He motioned that it would be all right, and I climbed up beside him. After I got used to the way he phrased his words, I understood him better and we had a very nice time for about ten minutes until I began to think about having him stop so I could get into the back seat as was proper. But he was already turning into what looked like a big park. There was a small white gatehouse in front of which he stopped. An officer came out and asked for my credentials.

"Where are we?" I asked the driver.

"This is the entrance to the castle," he told me.

There was no time to get out now. I told the officer on guard who I was and that I had an appointment with Her Majesty at ten o'clock. He went to telephone the castle and returned smiling.

"Her Majesty is expecting Fru Bjorn," he said.

We drove on through the beautiful trees and there stood the castle in the summer sun. We stopped in front of the many steps leading to the main entrance. Two men in white stood at the bottom of the steps, and two men in white were at the top. The Queen's Lady-in-Waiting came hurrying down to meet us. I felt a little funny sitting up on that high front seat with the driver. He did not even offer to help me down. He just sat there, so I climbed down myself and clasped the hand of the Lady-in-Waiting. She was very sweet and genuinely warm. The two men at the base bowed all the way to the ground and so did the men on the top step. She took me in through the door and we walked down a long corridor.

As we were walking along, I wondered what was the proper manner of greeting the Queen. Why hadn't I asked? Perhaps I should ask this lovely lady; she'd surely know. But just as I was about to speak, she turned to me.

"Here comes Her Majesty down the hall now to meet Fru Bjorn."

And there she was, as sweet and plain as any other lady. She was smiling and her steps were light. We stood there a second facing each other. Then I reached out my hand, and as I held hers, I curtsied. There was something about her, even in her simplicity, that demanded a curtsy. She took me by the arm and we walked past many rooms until she ushered me into a beautiful sitting room, called the blue room. It was a cosy room with many pictures of the royal family, some with inscriptions, much like those we have at home. I was seated at a small round table and the Queen seated herself opposite me.

She was dressed simply in a voile dress, with one strand of pearls, low shoes, no earrings, and wore only a couple of rings. Her hair was softly waved, combed back on the sides with a small knot at the nape of her neck. But I was not so conscious of what she wore as I was of her manner. Even in her sweetness there was a certain dignity—in the way she held her head and hands, the way she talked and smiled; the greatness of this woman shone through, and I was not at all disappointed. She was every bit a queen!

She made it easy to talk to her and we chatted about America, Sweden, and our families.

"How long have you been in America?" she asked me.

"Since nineteen twenty-four. You have been in America as long as I have been in Sweden."

After a while she took me for a walk outside the castle. She pointed to the ocean. "There is a lovely beach down there," she said. "I don't swim any more, but I used to. Years ago I swam every day."

The grounds were lovely everywhere I looked.

When we returned to the living room, I presented my book without my practiced speech. I just handed it to her. She thanked me and looked delighted. I told her a little about it and why I had written it.

"I love to read books like that." She smiled.

"Has Your Majesty ever been in America?" I asked.

"I was there last year; I traveled incognito. I visited Boston for a short time."

Suddenly I looked at the clock on the mantel; I had been there over a half an hour. I stood up.

"I must go!" I said.

She urged me to sit down. "Not yet, Fru Bjorn, stay a bit longer. I have absolutely nothing to do."

I stayed another half hour and then we walked down the corridor again, the men in white bowing here and there. The Queen walked with me all the way down the steps and there stood my taxi. I had no intention of climbing up into the front seat again. But I need not have worried. As we came walking down those steps, the driver got out of his car and stood by the back door. He even took my arm and helped me in. He certainly had changed. Perhaps it was the presence of the Queen that did it? I shook hands with Queen Louise and her Lady-in-Waiting again, and thanked Her Majesty for this wonderful morning.

"It was my pleasure." She smiled.

I rolled down the window, wanting to keep sight of her as long as I could. I heard her say to the Lady-in-Waiting as we drove off, "She has two daughters and two little grandsons."

I wanted so much to be friendly, but I didn't know if it was the proper thing to do. I followed my impulse. I leaned out the taxi window and waved at the Queen of Sweden. She smiled again and waved back. It made me so happy. I shall always remember that day, seeing her so lovely in her simplicity, so natural and friendly. I was glad Sweden had a queen like that, and I was thinking just that as we drove out on the lovely parkway under the big trees and among the hundreds of flowers. We passed the little white gatehouse. The gates opened and shut after us. The momentous visit was over, but I would never be quite the same again. I knew I had grown because I had met such a gracious lady.

My plans included a trip to Denmark, Holland, and England before returning to America; but first, the committee was to meet once more for a time of fellowship and to compare notes on what had happened since we parted. We had dinner in a hotel in Gothenburg. Someone tipped off the orchestra that there was a group of American ladies present, and that it would be appropriate to play an American tune. They did! They played "My Old Kentucky Home" and the music seemed to engulf the dining room; it laughed and cried and caressed us and my whole beautiful world seemed to turn upside down.

Suddenly a great homesickness crept up on me, a homesickness for America. A tear rolled slowly down my cheek. I could not explain how it happened, but it was as though I had awakened after a long sleep. I knew that Sweden was not my homeland any more; America was my home. I wanted to go back as soon as I could. I wanted to see The Star-Spangled Banner waving in the blue. I longed for the lakes and fields and mountains. At first it was hard for me to believe it, but my heart knew it was so. My ties with the old had been severed; my last roots had been pulled up. I was not divided any more; I was a whole person. I was as much an American as anyone born there. I belonged because as a citizen I had given my allegiance to America. I wanted to live there; I wanted to die there. I was going home to love America more than ever. In a dear little town, my new home stood waiting for me and my loved ones were there, counting the days until I returned. How wonderful life was! How blessed I had been! I was glad I had taken this journey and had met the people, and had had the experiences. It would be a memory that would stay with me always. But I was most grateful for this last experience, for the music that had awakened my heart.

Life has so much to offer if only we dare to take

what it has to give, and I would return home now to dream greater dreams of writing more books. How glad I was that I had learned that wonderful secret—to dare to dream.

~8

I am glad that I waited a couple of years before I began my second book, glad because I needed that interim to enjoy the miracle which had come into my life. A heart can only take in so much before it is filled to the top, pressed down and running over. And so it was during 1955, while I waited for the publication of my first book. When in September it was released and the letters and telegrams of congratulation came from so many well-meaning people, I needed time to hold everything to my heart and to thank God for it all again and again.

How amazed I was at the letters. It was like Christmas every day of the week! People loved *Papa's Wife!* They told me so!

Those very letters caused me to write *Papa's Daughter.* So many people wanted to know if I was Button, the naughty one, in *Papa's Wife.* Would I tell them some of the sins I committed in the parsonage? I answered letter after letter, revealing one or two things from my youth. I didn't have to do this, but the people who took the trouble to write to me because they were interested in my book became a part of my life; and I wanted to answer them, to give them what they wanted. But soon there were too many letters. I did not have the time to write and tell what a naughty little girl I had been.

So, one night I said to my husband, "I'm not going to answer letters about Button any more. I'll write her story and call it *Papa's Daughter*."

So another book was born!

Writing a book is much like having a baby. You conceive an idea and then share it with the other you, the creative one, and one day you know you are pregnant with a book. It is a glorious feeling to see that story develop step by step. You know just about when it will be completed and you set a date with your publisher for the birth of your book. You look forward to that date and count the days. You see progress during those months. The galleys come for you to proofread and the jacket arrives. My books had such lovely jackets! The artist who creates them is a contributor to that unborn book.

It took me exactly nine months to write *Papa's Daughter*. I did not use an agent now; perhaps because I was so independent. But because I couldn't be bothered with sentence structure and spelling, I needed a helper, and with this new book my sister Ann did the correcting. I'll bet she laughed many times as she read my words. Sometimes she would write and ask, "What kind of a word is that in the second chapter, third page, third line? It's not Swedish and it's not English, but I think I know what you mean and I have changed it to a word that really exists."

I never tried to change my English. I loved the freedom of writing my own way. That was one thing I had decided from the beginning; there would be no walls or fences around me; I would remain completely free. There were times when Ann and I argued a little over minor points, perhaps because Ann was well educated. I, on the other hand, had never learned much from books and I had never gone to school in America except to those evening courses which many immigrants attended two nights a week. But Ann usually won because in my heart I knew she was right. Yet, I was always sure of my meaning and that was good, for without self-confidence I could have accomplished nothing.

It was in the spring of 1957 that I began to work on *Papa's Daughter*. It was to be released on April 26, 1958—my oldest brother's birthday. When *Papa's Wife* had so appropriately come out on my birthday, I had decided to make this a tradition; each of my books would come out on the birthday of someone close.

Spring, that time when the long, cold winter is replaced by new life, would be a good birthday for my second book. I looked forward to it. The summer of 1957 I went to Canada for a retreat. It seemed easier for me to create there, surrounded by inspirational people who had, like myself, journeyed to a quiet place, seeking rest for their minds and souls. It was in Whitby, Canada, that I wrote the chapter, "The Angel," about the baby I had never held in my arms, about that first real grief in my young life. I never could have written that story if I had not been in that atmosphere of love and prayer. After that chapter had been written, the sorrow I had carried for my first baby left me and my mind was filled with happy thoughts about her. That fall the book was completed.

"You will never feel the same thrill with the second book that you did with the first," an established author told me one day. "After you have written a number of books, it becomes just a matter of fact. The thrill never comes back."

But she was wrong; the thrill was the same for me with each new book. Just like children, they are alive. They're not just words; each book has its own disposition, its own self.

Very often I am asked, "Tell me, Mrs. Bjorn, which of your books do you like best yourself?"

I never hesitate. It is so easy to answer.

"How many children do you have?" I asked one lady who put that question to me.

She smiled proudly. "I have five boys," she said.

"And which one do you like best?"

She looked perplexed for a moment, and then a light came into her eyes.

"Oh, I see what you mean. Your books *are* like children to you. You like each one as much as the others."

That was exactly what I wanted to get across. Each one of my books was a part of me; they were the evidence of the thoughts, the love, the beauty which I myself had experienced. They are alive!

Someone else said one day, "Aren't you afraid that some person will steal your style? You have such a unique way of expressing yourself."

"No one could," I said firmly. "I don't believe that anyone can steal what your heart creates. Even if someone tries to imitate, that work would not have the same spirit in it."

I don't worry about these things. I feel that every person who is born to create has his own rhythm. It's like the tune of a song which sings within you. And if a prospective author can find his own rhythm through my creations, he has my blessings to start from there and go ahead. The finished product would never be exactly the same. Even the snowflakes which God has created have individual designs.

I had much joy from *Papa's Daughter* and I often gave talks based on my second book. I was still traveling around the country for the Redpath Bureau. One day I was invited to speak at an author's luncheon at G. Fox and Company in neighboring Hartford, Connecticut. There were other authors there and I was delighted to sit and listen to their experiences, which had been, in a way, so different from mine. They were people who devoted their lives to writing. To me, writing was a side line, a hobby; I wrote for the fun of writing and for the wonder of creating. But my real life was in my home with my husband and younger daughter who was now in college and much in need of a mother to set her straight at times. My older daughter and her children lived nearby. There were only two lovely grandsons then, but they filled so much of my heart. I wanted the best part of my life to go to all of them first, but I admit that my writing did take some of my time away from them. Still I considered it only a hobby.

But that day in Hartford, the lectures were followed by a question-and-answer period.

It was then I was asked, "How does your husband like your books?"

I answered, as always, honestly and perhaps, at that time, not thinking of the results.

"I don't know," I laughed. "I don't think my husband reads my books."

People gasped, but it was true. I think that Bob feels he would be embarrassed at the strange things I say about the family, although I do very often read a chapter to him when I'm writing it. But when a book is ready, he just holds it in his hand and perhaps tells me that the cover is attractive. But I've never seen him take one to read. It could be that he reads them when I don't know about it, although I doubt that.

Well, to my surprise, when the Hartford newspaper came out the next day, there was quite a bit on the author's luncheon, but the headline nearly knocked me over. It read: "Author's Husband Never Reads His Wife's Books."

If there's anything my Bob hates, it's publicity in any form. He is a quiet, reserved man, and his own life and what he thinks and does are plainly his own business. I know he would have been furious had he seen the paper. I should know by now that he does not like personal publicity. How I hurried that day to all the local stores which I thought handled Hartford papers. I spent a good deal of money buying them up, I assure you; then I clipped one article, placed it in a secure place, and dumped the rest in the trash. I'm pretty sure Bob never read the article and no one mentioned it to him; and unless he reads this book, that episode will remain an undiscovered sin which his wife committed.

After that I tried to be more careful and think a

thing through before saying it. I'm getting better. I don't reveal everything that happens at home. But let me put it this way—I've learned that it's not always easy to be both a wife and an author if you're writing homespun philosophy.

The many letters which arrived each day thrilled me, but they also consumed a lot of my time. I loved each letter, not because it was written to me about my books, but because through these correspondents I understood that those books had become a part of many people's lives. The people had confidence in me and wanted to add a little personal touch by writing to me.

The letters from the young touched my heart most. I realized how lonely they were. I had had that lonely feeling too when I was a teenager. I remember how often when I was appearing the gayest, that sudden feeling swept over me, right in the middle of everything—the feeling that I didn't belong there, that I didn't belong anywhere. I used to slip away and go out into the garden, put my arms around a tree, and cry my heart out. The next day it was all forgotten and I was happy again. The young slip into these moods without knowing why. They don't know it is just a part of growing up. Moving from childhood into youth is a terrific task. I think as they read *Papa's Daughter,* they felt a sense of kinship; they knew that I knew what it was to be young. Some of the letters were truly unique, such as this one:

Dear Button,

I call you Button because you are so close to me. I have laughed and cried with your story and suddenly it is my story too. May I talk to you sometime? No one understands me, but I think you would. You are real, Button. If only you had been a teenager now and been my friend, what pals we would have been. You did not belong way back there. You belong to our time because you are just like me. But I did not mean to write all this. I was

67

only going to thank you for writing this wonderful book and please write some more.

I love you,
Jan

I smiled as I read it and a little prayer went up to God for Jan. I wrote her a nice long letter. After hearing from her many times, I know there is wonderful material in that teenager. There was so much that she never actually told me, but I could read a lot between the lines.

The next letter was very different.

Dear Mrs. Bjorn,
I have read your book *Papa's Daughter* and I would like to know some things about it. Did you enjoy doing naughty things? Why did you write about them? Was it supposed to teach children to be naughty? I think you were a scream, and even if you are more interesting being bad, I am glad you turned out good.

Very truly yours,
Betty

That letter took me a little longer to answer. Betty did not lay her heart bare as Jan had. But perhaps my book would influence Betty more. My answer would be very important, because on that I would be judged by her and followed, I hoped.

When letters like that reached me, I knew that the written word was very important; and after *Papa's Daughter,* I knew that whatever I wrote would be read by thousands of people and that some of them would be influenced by my books, influenced for the good. And this letter was proof of that very thing.

Dear Mrs. Bjorn,
I picked up your book *Papa's Daughter* in the library because I had read your first book and the family was now like my closest friend. I cried and

laughed with Button, and I liked the way she always prayed. I had never prayed; I thought it was silly. But I tried to pray like Button prayed, and God heard my prayer. Now I pray all the time, and it has made me very happy. I have a new life because of a book you have written.

Sincerely,
Elenore

I was thrilled with all these letters and so grateful. Perhaps, I was thinking, my books can be a beacon for some people lost in darkness. It allowed me, in a sense, to continue with my Papa's work. The ministry is not only carried on from the pulpit of a church; it speaks to people in the beauty of nature and the roar of the storm, the calm of a sunset, in all creative arts that inspire good. I am sure that those thoughts planted a tiny seed in my heart and the idea of a new book had begun, a book that in spite of its simplicity would bring the greatest joy to me. And once again I would stand amazed at what words can accomplish.

∾9

My third book, *Mama's Way*, was done unexpectedly and much sooner than I ever thought I could write a book. My mind had toyed with the idea that, in a couple of years after *Papa's Daughter*, I would write another family story. I think those ideas naturally live in an author's mind because people are always asking, "Are you working on another book? What is it going to be about this time?" And as parents like to have their children come with at least a couple of years between them, so an author likes to have her books come out at regular intervals. Yet, once in a while there is a surprise—the unexpected child who comes much sooner than planned. But often that one brings more comfort in later life than all the other children put together. This was the case of my third book.

Mama's Way took me only six months to write. Although *Papa's Daughter* was less than one year old (born in April, 1958), by January, 1959, this religious book was already published. I was grateful that my publisher was willing and happy to accept this book which was so different from the other two.

I had never planned to write a book like this one. It wasn't that I did not want to write a spiritual book; it was that I didn't feel worthy of doing it. Having a brother who is a theologian and who has written many books on religion, I, who had never taken a course in religion nor studied theology, felt I was not equipped to write on that subject. I knew my brother Nels would never object, because he is not like that. He is wonderful and sweet in every way, one of those truly great Christians. But how could I attempt something I was not trained for? It was a minister who challenged me to do this, and I shall always be grateful that he saw that I had the quality to write a successful spiritual book. And God blessed it. He blessed it more than I had ever dared to dream.

Now as I look back on those years which have passed since I became an author, I can see why this book had to be written just at that time. I know that God led every step of the way and that He poured down special blessings on my efforts. I needed that book myself. One day I was going to have to turn to it when a great tragedy came into my own life. I would have to stand the test as to whether what I had written really existed—that one, as a mortal, can leave everything with God and never take it back; that one can make one's own disappointments into His appointments; that one can know without a shadow of a doubt that he stands on a rock which cannot be moved. I learned all of this and more. My book was a written creed of the way I wanted to live always here in my earthlife.

So often people have said to me, "Whatever makes you so religious? You don't seem like one of those people until I begin to talk with you, but somehow I always end up talking about something in the religious field."

And I answer that it is because my religion is more than a creed, more than something I try to live up to. My religion is me; it is as much a part of me as my heartbeat, my sight, or my hearing. I would not be a whole, balanced, happy person without it. It was planted in me by my Mama before I was born. Mama felt that her children were not really hers; they were only loaned to her by God. And when she was sure she was with child, she gave that child back to God, promising that she would do her best to plant the seeds of right living in its heart as soon as it could understand things. And Papa nurtured that planting. He disciplined it and made it strong. There was no compromising with my Papa. Religion was not sold cheaply; it was not pushed back into a corner to be taken out only at certain times. Religion, to Papa, was an expensive item, something to be respected, glorified, and held high. I was, indeed, a very blessed child to have parents like that, and because of this richer life within me, I have found the secret of true happiness.

I know that when my book came out, some of the big newspapers did not review it; and that many people were disappointed that an author who had so much humor in her had suddenly begun to write about prayer. But I forgave them, because they did not understand. I had no way of explaining to them that the world needed *Mama's Way*. Now a trunkful of letters would prove that this book reached out a helping hand to many, giving them peace and comfort.

Just yesterday I met a nurse in the hospital who stopped me and said, "Mrs. Bjorn, I want to tell you something strange. A patient of mine has just finished your book, *Mama's Way*, which she got from the hospital library. She was the most tiresome, querulous person I have ever seen, but your book changed her. She claims it gave her a faith, and now for the first time in life she is happy."

Nothing in the world could please me more than to hear those words, because what our world needs today is faith. As a Christian nation we have shown our philosophy to the world in a very poor manner. America needs a jubilant, strong, unmovable faith in God to set the rest of the world an example. We will never do it with bombs and war and terror, but by showing God's love and a strong faith in the good.

Perhaps the greatest miracle was that my book was

accepted among Catholics as well as Protestants. It spoke to all in their own tongue. My first letter from an unknown Catholic friend came from Little Rock, Arkansas. This lady wrote: "For the first time in my life I am reaching out my hand to a Protestant to say, 'You surely have found Him as I have found Him.' " She was the editor of a Catholic newspaper and quoted me many times in her articles. We corresponded for a while, and I found her to be a wonderful person.

Then came a letter from a man who for years had studied for the priesthood, then had given up in his last year to become a teacher instead. He was writing a book about his experiences and one day I hope to see it published. His religion meant the world to him; yet he claimed that my book made him a stronger Catholic. He said that he had not understood prayer until he read my book.

He wrote, "Your simple little book made me see things so clearly, things I had not understood before. I finished at two o'clock one morning. I was thrilled. All that I had studied and tried to cram down in my heart during my years in the theological school suddenly came to life. I knew I had never known how to pray. My prayers had just been a repetition of words. But now I know, and my faith is growing by leaps and bounds."

I had many letters from him. I was invited to his home for many delightful meals and met his lovely little family. He is a fine man, a great asset to his country. Although our theology is different, we find a complete unity of spirit.

And I have learned this, that Christians have lost much ground by bickering among themselves as to who is right and who is wrong instead of uniting as a strong force against evil. There is no time for this sort of thing, and the ecumenical movement now in progress will leave a greater impact on the world than all our space ships. We live in great times.

My spiritual book opened new doors for me, new fields. I was asked to speak at retreats and conferences,

73

and many times ministers have wanted special sessions when we could sit and talk for hours about what we could do to help our world become a different place, one led by the Prince of Peace. Many times I preached at churches, when the minister stepped down and gave me his pulpit. Perhaps some people think I should have refused, that I should have known better, but the minister asked me and I always felt there was a reason for my being asked. Perhaps something I said about God would be planted and bear fruit. As long as I didn't try to prepare, as long as I knew the right words would be given to me, I had nothing to fear. My unwritten sermons surprised me many times over. But once I almost failed at a very important moment.

I was in the Chicago area, giving talks mostly in churches. One engagement was to preach the evening sermon in a church in one of the fashionable suburbs of that great city. I took for granted that it was a small church and I wasn't worried. I would know what to say when the time came. I had so much to share. But when I arrived, I found that it was a large church, with two pastors, and filled with about five hundred people anticipating an inspiring sermon.

As the pastor stepped down and I took my place behind the pulpit, I said to myself, "Thyra, you are a fool! How do you get yourself into these things? What are you going to say to all those people? You don't even have any notes to guide you!"

There seemed to be nowhere to begin. And then suddenly I knew what had happened. Because of the magnitude of the church, I wanted to be a sensation. Well, I was no minister. I only spoke as the words came. They had asked *me* to come, and I needed only to be myself. Fear could have no room in my heart. Didn't the Master whom I was serving choose the simple fishermen to be his followers and broadcast the good news? And so I looked down at the people and smiled, saying: "My first memory of my childhood was a parsonage, a parsonage where a pastor lived with his

74

wife and eight children. Mama and Papa brought us up on prayer . . ."

And from that point on the words just came. Later when I was greeting the people, I knew that they were not disappointed. I had preached their evening message in a unique way perhaps, but God had blessed my words and their souls had been reached. After that, I promised myself never to feel I must impress anyone; I must always remember just to be *me,* no matter what the circumstance.

My third book had just come out and had been selling well everywhere in America when something happened to our happy, secure homelife. The summer of 1959 was an unhappy one. A home was at stake; a marriage was breaking up. There had never been a divorce in our family; a thing like that was never even considered. When we children of Papa and Mama took a mate, it was for life! People say that times have changed and that divorce is not as bad as it used to be in the sight of people, but rationalizing does not lessen this blight that has come on the younger generation of today. Divorce is never right; it leaves its mark on the innocent and breaks down something which can never be built again.

My older daughter had married too early in life. Her husband was a fine boy and came from a good family, but they could not get along together. They tried to make each other over from the beginning and that was wrong. Freedom is such a precious thing and the respect of each other's freedom is essential. When one tries to rule the other's thoughts, a wall is built which will someday fall and crush those behind it. Their wall crashed one day! Four little children stood wide-eyed wondering what had caused the storm to come into their young lives. There was nothing I could do to still the storm because it was raging just as strongly in my own heart. After their separation, there was a long period of adjustment. The wound took a long time to heal. But it did, leaving, of course, an ugly scar. But thanks be to God, our grandchildren are growing up in security now. They are growing up to be fine American citizens. There is so much to be grateful for. I found a new philosophy for those dark days and I tried to say it aloud each new morning, "This too will pass."

I turned time and time again to my own book and found that what I had prescribed for my readers was the thing I leaned on so heavily myself, and it was strong and secure. And I remembered Mama and what she told me just when it seemed the darkest around me. I telephoned her in Miami and told her what was about to take place. I would have loved to save her from this heartbreak; she was old now. Why couldn't all this have waited until her earth time was up? I was afraid of what it would do to her. But Mama, as she had so often before, astonished me with her calmness and serenity.

"Thyra, remember this," she said firmly. "God can take the worst mess and make beauty out of it."

Did Mama see into the future? Could she predict what was to come? It seems so because there was a second marriage for both of them. Happiness did come and soon the darkness will be completely displaced by this new light.

I suppose this is all a part of life. Who am I that I should escape the sorrow and grief and worry which come to us all on earth's journey? I grew a great deal, and I knew again how strong the everlasting arms are that reach down from Heaven to earth.

I received more letters about *Mama's Way* than both the other books together. I had to set right those many people who felt that I had an *in* with God. They believed that if I prayed for them their prayers would be heard. I had to make them understand that He is not my God alone; He is a Father to all who seek Him and their own prayers would reach Him as fast as mine. And letters came from all places, from all ages, letters such as these:

Dear Mrs. Bjorn,

I have read your book *Mama's Way,* and I will never be the same person again. I am going to start living right now. There is so much for me to do. I want to set my life straight. I want to begin anew to be the best wife and mother, and to be a friend to the lonely. When I read it, it was as though a spark touched me, and I wanted God more than anything else in life. Perhaps that is what it means to thirst after righteousness. God bless you, and if I live a hundred years, I couldn't thank you enough for what your book has done for me.

Sincerely yours,
Katherine Gossardt

One little girl of about twelve years wrote me:

Dear Mrs. Bjorn,

When I came to page 72 of your book *Mama's Way,* I began to cry. That is not so unusual, but I also began to pray and that is something I had never done before . . .

That was just a part of the letter. There are too many even to try to include a fraction of them in this book. I often feel that *Mama's Way* was my graduation. I learned so much from my own heart, and I learned to speak to all denominations, each one claiming that it was his religion about which I had written. I know from that, that one day all men can be brothers. We can agree to disagree and we can love each other in spite of the different ways we have been brought up and the different doctrines which have been planted in our hearts. We cannot change these things that fence us in. The color of one's skin and the language one speaks should not keep us apart. We cannot help where we were born or who our parents were or the walls that have been raised by prejudice; but we can break down the walls and tear down the fences, and respect and love each other, building around our world a circle of love on which we must all work together, hand in hand, if it is going to be completed.

I am grateful for this book and I know I will aways consider it my greatest.

10

It was during my visit to Sweden in 1956 that I bought my native costume which would be used exclusively for lecturing. The idea had been very appealing to me as I realized more and more how very pronounced my Swedish accent was. Once when I had spoken to a large gathering in the vicinity of my home town, the mayor of Springfield, Massachusetts, had been in the audience. After the lecture, he complimented me with these words:

"I enjoyed every moment of your fine talk. You are very clever. My own parents came from Sweden and I would give anything to be able to put on a Swedish accent like that."

I could feel a slight blush coming to my face. "Thank you," I replied, "but I would give anything to get rid of it."

After that, my accent bothered me more than ever. At times I tried to warn people by telling them that I spoke with an accent. Then one afternoon, after I had spoken to a women's club, a very sweet old lady told me that there was no need for me to take the time to tell them about my accent.

"The minute you start talking," she informed me bluntly, "we all know."

All these incidents made me decide to put a label on myself. If I dressed in a Swedish costume, people would expect an accent; in fact, they would be very disappointed if I didn't have one. That really solved my problem and people were delighted when I appeared in my colorful, hand-embroidered costume; and it did add atmosphere to my talks.

I selected the prettiest of all the Swedish costumes— A *floda-dräkt* from the province of Dalarna. It is true that I was born in Lapland and that I should have bought a Lap costume, but it was not as becoming to me as the Dalarna one, so I figured: Why not wear the prettiest one? As a daughter of Sweden, I had a right to choose any costume from the many which were available, and mine has proven very effective. Yet it has also served another purpose.

I had never wanted authorship to interfere with my homelife. Over and over again I told myself that I must never change. I must never let my Bob and the girls feel that I had become another person because I had a career. That career must never become more than a hobby. I was a wife and mother first; they were my primary duties. I loved keeping house. I adored the arts of cleaning, washing, cooking, and entertaining, which I called "playing house." I could remember when I was six or seven years old, I had a secret corner in the parsonage garden where I had a playhouse. I had pieces of broken glass or dishes, and leaves, roots, and bark for food; but, oh, how I worked and cooked and cleaned. I was never happier than when I was all alone in my playhouse.

I had never lost that sense of play. Keeping house, to me, is still a happy game. Our home is a dear, cozy place that we all love. It is the place we return to after a day at school or work or lecturing. It is love and security. I wanted it always to have the odor of something extra good cooking or baking; I wanted it always to have a table set with flowers or something green, even in midwinter. I wanted always to have a bowl of fruit on top of the refrigerator, flowers on the table, and a bright light in the window at night when the family returned. Home must always be the dearest place in the world, and the place in which I am queen. It means far more to me than all the books in the world.

But as a lecturer, I had to get into the mood for speaking. My costume was a wonderful inspiration. The moment I changed into it, I left my housewifely duties and became an author. For a while the home with its many responsibilities was completely forgotten and I gave myself entirely to telling stories and entertaining people.

In 1959 I gave up speaking for the Redpath Bureau. It had been a part of my life for which I shall ever be grateful. Through the Bureau I had earned a reputation as a lecturer and became known in a large part of America. They took me on as an unknown housewife before my book had found a publisher, and I owe them a great part of my success.

But after the publication of *Mama's Way,* my life changed. To travel around telling funny stories was not enough for me. I had seen how a speaker could capture an audience, how she could move them to laughter, how she could move them to tears, and how she could make them forget their troubles and burdens and see them leave, renewed people.

Once after a talk a man came up to me—a big, strong, he-man type. He shook my hand and said, "Mrs. Bjorn, tell me your secret. How can you bring tears to the eyes of a strong, hardhearted man like me?"

It has happened so often. One minute I would have people screaming with laughter and the next minute wiping the tears from their cheeks. My speaking, as well as my writing, is a gift from God. These two fine talents He had planted in me and I wanted to use them to capacity. While formerly I had enjoyed speaking to large clubs and organizations, I now wanted to devote my energy to churches and smaller groups. I wanted

81

the freedom to give my time, if need be, without obligation to anyone. So a new era of my life began, different fields and different missions. I have never once regretted this step. It is true that the money was not the same, but money means little when it comes to happiness. To be able to help people onto the straight path of life, to lighten a burden and give some discouraged one hope and peace of mind means more to me than money. I traveled thousands of miles and met more and more people, but I always found that in every place there was one person who needed me.

One time I spoke in a small town in New Jersey, to a small group of people. I had traveled a long, long way; and I wondered, as I closed, why I was there. Shaking hands with the people as they left, I noticed that a young boy had lingered. I think he was about eighteen years old—a fine, strong lad. He held my hand for a long time and then he bent and kissed it. There were tears in his eyes when he looked at me again.

"Mrs. Bjorn," he said, "I don't know just how to thank you for your talk. I've been so bewildered through my school years. I've tried to settle in my mind what I should become, but I couldn't find the answer. I have found it tonight. I am the happiest I have been in years. I am going into the ministry; it is clear to me now. God has given me a talent, too, a talent for reaching people. I can't wait to get started."

He walked out with the others and disappeared. I have never seen him since, but my heart bubbled over with joy because I knew what was planted of God would grow and bear fruit for His Kingdom.

So often when I meet people I sense their need. Once in Chicago I met a very lovely lady. As I shook her hand and looked into her eyes, there was a world of sorrow in them. Her lips smiled as she spoke to me, but her eyes told the story. I said to her, "Have you time to wait a moment? I'd like to present you with my book, *Mama's Way*."

"She looked surprised, but she lingered and we talked for a while.

"I'd love to have your book," she confided, "but I have no money with me tonight."

"My book is a little gift to you," I said.

"But why?" she asked. "I don't know you. I'm not even a member of this church. I just dropped in because I had nothing else to do tonight."

"You take my book," I urged. "I don't know why, but I have a strange desire to give it to you."

She left with the book clasped in her hand. I wondered about the incident. Who was she? Why did she need the book? What was her sorrow? Yet, even if I never knew these things, I knew I had done the right thing. So I remembered her on my long prayer list and went on to other places.

Then one night when I was to speak at another church in Chicago, I was given an address where I was to spend the night. When I arrived, I was told that the lady had had to leave town unexpectedly and was given a new address. When I rang the bell at the new address, the very lady to whom I had given the book answered the door.

"When I knew you were coming to our church," she said, "I wanted so very much to have you in my home. I need so desperately to have someone to talk to. My whole world has tumbled down these last few months. I have prayed about it. You said in your talk and in your book that if we talk to God as a Father, He will answer. Then out of a clear, blue sky, I had a phone call asking if I would open my home to you as your hostess had suddenly been called out of town. You can imagine how thrilled and grateful I was. And here you are when I need you so very, very much."

She did need someone. I was happy to be the one. There was a broken home; I knew what she was going through. We spent a couple of wonderful days together. I have not heard from her since, but that is not my field. God has ordained it this way. One plants the seed; one cultivates and waters it; one trusts that there will be ripe fruit.

I shall never forget that trip to Chicago. One night

there I did get the scare of my life. I was again looking for an address, and by some mistake I had been given the wrong one. As I drove through the streets of that big city approaching a certain area, I suddenly realized that this was not a very nice neighborhood. I wondered why the church had placed me in a home in this section; but in my field, you just have to know in your heart that there is a reason for everything and not ask too many questions. The house I entered had a few steps missing; the windows were curtainless and dirty. It was an awful place, and I was really frightened. When I pressed the bell, it made no sound. There were voices, loud voices from somewhere in the house; but no one came to the door. I waited a moment and then hurried away. How relieved I felt taking long strides over the missing steps. I never wanted to return there again.

The house next door had a patch of garden in the back yard and a woman was scratching in it with a hoe. I walked up to her and asked for information concerning the people next door. Of course, their name was different from the one I had been given. I asked if I might use her telephone to call the church where I was to speak to report the mistake. The lady was kind and ushered me into her living room where the telephone stood on a table in a dark corner. I found a telephone book, called the number of the church and learned the right address.

Just as I put down the receiver, a bedroom door pushed open slowly and a man with a revolver appeared in the doorway. He did not point the gun at me. He did not speak. He just stood there staring at me.

I must admit, I had never been so frightened. I even forgot to pray for help. My blood seemed to turn to ice. Here I was in an undesirable part of Chicago, a woman in a strange house, with an unknown man holding a gun. The woman had returned to her garden, and I tried to take a step in the direction of the back door, but the man stepped in front of me.

"Lady, we have a front door," he said, cracking a smile.

I tried to smile back. "But I always go out the way I came in."

I hoped he wouldn't see my legs shaking. He didn't say another word. Bravely I kept smiling and walked past him, opened what I thought was the back door, and stepped into a large closet. The man still said nothing. Somehow I scrambled out of the closet and opened the right door, and went out into the back yard, happy and relieved, but shaking like a leaf in the wind. I finally made it to my car. Never had it felt so good to be there, to lock the door, to step on the gas, and to drive away.

But as I drove past a car in front of me, I noticed something printed on its door. I slowed down long enough to read it. "Stockyard Police," it read. Suddenly I laughed out loud. That was all there was to it. The man was a policeman. He was probably going to work. Perhaps he was only going to put his revolver in its holster. He was not dangerous at all. Just because the neighborhood was not the best, the people were not necessarily bad. But I was glad to leave and drive to a better part of the city, to find the correct address with a pleasant room in which to collapse until I could become my happy self again.

I marvel when I think of the amount of traveling I do and how I have been protected on my tours and my everyday driving. One flat tire is the only trouble I have had with my car in all these years, even driving through ice and fog and snow. I am seldom afraid, for I know that I have a power which surrounds me wherever I am, so that nothing can happen to me without God's permission. Because each new day I give my life into His keeping and care, I live only for that one day. Yesterday is gone. Tomorrow I have not seen. But for today God has promised that as your day, so shall your strength be. I rest on that promise. Though evil comes, as it sometimes does, the good, when we steadfastly believe in it, is stronger. Once, I admit, I lost hold of

85

the good for a few minutes, but only for a few minutes. As soon as I took hold of it again, it held.

I was traveling outside Boston one lovely spring evening. I was going to Revere to speak at a Mother and Daughter Banquet. It was late and I had gotten onto a new road with no route numbers and, in spite of the fact that I was following my directions carefully, I had no idea of where I was going. Right and left I know, but east and west mean very little to me on an unfamiliar road. My directions were in terms of east and west, and I could easily have taken the wrong turn. It was a wide highway, at least four lanes—one of those highways on which you feel alone no matter how much traffic there is. There was no place to turn off and no gas stations at which to ask directions, so I pulled over to the side of the road and just sat there, hoping that someone would stop to see if I was in trouble. And it did not take long before a light truck pulled up in front of me and a man leaned out of the window.

"Are you in trouble, lady?" he called.

I smiled at him. "I'm afraid I'm lost. Can you please tell me if this is the road to Revere?"

He jumped out of the truck and came to my window on the driver's side. I had my pocketbook open because I had taken the directions from it and had not closed it. The pocketbook was full almost to overflowing with dollar bills. I had spoken way up in Vermont that same afternoon. They had charged one dollar for the tickets and when they gave me an honorarium, they had given it to me in one-dollar bills. Because I had left in a hurry, I had not taken the time to fold it and put it away. I had simply stuffed it into my pocketbook. I could see that the man's eyes focused on all that money, not seeing that it was in small bills. Before I had time to think, he was on the other side and in the car sitting beside me. But I had had time to put the pocketbook between me and the driver's door. He evidently missed the purse which had been on the seat, but he moved very close to me and put his arm around me. I tried to act nonchalant.

"I'm glad you can give me directions," I said. "I'm speaking at a banquet in Revere, and I'm late. These new roads get me confused."

"And you are very, very lost indeed," he said.

His breath smelled very strongly of liquor, and I noticed that his truck was a liquor truck.

Suddenly he asked, "What's the matter with your foot?"

I realized then that he must have discovered the pocketbook and wanted me to bend forward to look at my foot; but I did not move an inch.

"There's nothing the matter with my foot. I am feeling fine. All I want is to know where I am. You are kind to help me."

His arm tightened around me. His eyes gleamed wickedly, and suddenly I became very frightened. My chest was very tight, and my heart almost stopped beating; but I only had that feeling for a moment. There was no need for fear even with this awful man in the car beside me. I knew that God would help me.

"God," I prayed, "protect me from this man. Thank you for Your love."

His arm was still around me, but now it was as though his grip was frozen there. He did not move it. I tried to look gay and a little impish. I don't know where the thought came from or even how the words came, but I said to the man: "Is there a place near here where you and I could be alone?"

He tightened his arm around my shoulders. His rough cheek touched mine.

"Good girl," he said. "I know just the place. I'll drive the truck ahead and you follow me."

He jumped out of my car. I locked the door and started off. I didn't even give him a chance to get in front of me. I pushed the gas pedal to the floor, and there, just around the bend was a big sign—Revere.

My heart was pounding now. I drove to the church and gave my talk and stayed overnight in the home of a lovely lady. I slept well that night, but in the morning when I started to walk downstairs to breakfast, my legs just wouldn't hold me up. They were like paper folding under me—a delayed shock perhaps. The full force of the danger I had been in descended upon me. Before that I had just been filled with gratitude.

What if the man had insisted I drive him to the secluded spot? What if all the things that went through my brain had happened to me? Evil had been there in full force, but my faith had held; the minute I took hold of it, it worked.

I learned a lesson from that incident—never to leave my car door unlocked. It was a good lesson. What a lucky person I was and how blessed. But the memory of those moments and that man followed me for days afterward. I was so happy to return home again to the shelter of my own home and the love of my husband.

"It was an awful thing for you to go through," he said, "but now you will listen to what I have told you and keep your doors locked at all times."

I think perhaps it bothered him more than he let on. He did not want to frighten me more than I had been already. My Bob is such a wise man and so fine and understanding. It is good of him to let me do all this driving around the country. But I know that it is because he feels that I have a mission to fulfill and that the God we both love and serve will be my help in time of trouble.

~11

It was in 1961 that Mama began to talk about feeling old. She had turned eighty-one that March. Of course we knew that the years had changed her, that she had lost a lot of weight after her heart attack, that she didn't run to and fro as she used to, and that her face had hundreds of fine lines on it. But what Mama minded most was that her eyes had begun to fail her. When her dear letters came to us children, we could tell from the crooked lines that it was hard for her to see. Mama, who always planned for all the family, now began making plans for her last journey into eternity. She planned for it as though she were simply moving from one house to another. She cleaned out her belongings —destroying some, giving away others, and boxing those she wanted us to keep.

"I don't want anyone to have to come and clean out things I've accumulated," she told me one day. "It's better to do it yourself."

"Oh, Mama," I said, "you have lots of time yet. Don't talk as though you were ready to leave us now."

Mama laughed happily. "I like to talk about it, so that you get used to the idea. I want you to know that I was prepared and that I looked forward to a wonderful journey."

Yes, Mama set her house in order in plenty of time. Once when I was visiting her in Miami, she put her arm around me and said, "After I have left this earth, you must have no regrets, Thyra. Remember that. You've been a dear and wonderful daughter and so good to your Mama."

I am glad Mama told me that because I was to remember it many times. And the last time she flew east to visit us children who live there, we had no idea that she had arranged her affairs as though she would never return. And she didn't return. On a visit to her son Folke in Rochester, New York, her orders to leave earth came suddenly and without warning. After she had left us, we knew that Heaven was richer because she was there. The beauty of Mama's graduation lingered with us for a long, long time, hard as it was to accept the fact that we could no longer pick up the phone and hear the voice or receive her dear letters weekly. There was a great emptiness and yet none of us questioned God's wisdom concerning the day and the hour. We had had her a long time and she had been a part of our lives for many years. Through her letters we knew all about each other. Who would tell us now and who would remind us about a birthday or an anniversary or inform us that someone was ill? We didn't realize until after she had gone how very much she did for us.

But letters still came to me asking about Mama. Was she still alive? Was she well? Please tell us, because through your books she has become such a part of us.

So in 1962 I began to write my last book about the family, trying to make it a happy book containing the stories that Mama had told me about us children when we were small. It was such a joy writing about the past and living again the precious memories; I ended the book with Mama's passing into eternity. The book was published in the fall of 1963, and was written in memory of Mama. She would have loved that—a book rich with laughter and tears of joy and sorrow. It was the first time Mama had not read what I had written about her, but I could feel her approval; in my mind I could see her smile as she discovered how well I had remembered her stories. I had her blessing on *Dear Papa* and it was good for my heart, which still ached from the parting. This book would join the other three and sell just as well.

I was still busy with speaking and traveling and I met many wonderful people wherever I went. Soon it seemed to me that the whole wide world was my family. I have a way of feeling at home wherever I am. As soon as I step inside a door, I am part of the family. It is the variety of this life that I love and its many surprises; this is the spark that keeps me on the go. I have never kept track of the number of times I have spoken or the number of people I have met; I don't like to think in figures. I do not always remember names, not even the names of those people in whose homes I have been a guest, but I do remember faces. Some homes, voices, and incidents are still clear in my mind; these are mostly the little things, but they make up the treasures I have gathered here on earth and they will warm my heart forever. How much wider my horizon is now and how much more I know about people than I did when I first began traveling. There is so much love, thoughtfulness, and goodness in people. I'm glad I have learned this from my contact with them.

People often ask, "Do you travel alone? Do you drive those hundreds of miles to new places without a companion?"

No, I don't travel alone, and I never lack a companion. Wherever I go, God is with me. I have no fear as I start out because I know that my life is in God's hand. I am sure of His love and His protection. It is such a wonderful feeling. I never start off without a prayer. When I stay overnight in someone's home, I kneel by the bed in which I have slept and pray that God will bless and repay these people for their kindness to me. It seems strange to some people, but not to me, that if I travel into a complex city where it is very difficult to find my destination, there is always someone sent to guide me just when I need them. But at times I do get into trouble.

Recently I had traveled about five hundred and twenty-five miles one day to reach a camp in the woods of a strange state. It was almost dark and I should have been worried, but as always I never doubted that I would find the place. However, I was very tired. When I reached the small village where I was to make a particular turn around a traffic circle, instead of going around the big circle, I turned too soon and went the wrong way through what seemed to be a small park. Every car I met blew its horn at me.

What a friendly town, I thought, and soon the police chief himself was there blinking his light at me. How friendly, I thought . . . and how nice . . . now I can ask him about the road. I stopped in the middle of the street to meet the cruiser.

"I am so glad I met you." I smiled. "I am looking for a certain road into a Bible camp in the woods. Now I can ask you where to go."

He glared at me. "I was about to ask you where you thought you were going," he snapped. "Can't you read signs? There is a big one where you turned. It says: Do Not Enter!"

I was a little taken back. The smile faded away; there was a lump in my throat. I was so tired and it was getting dark.

"I am so sorry," I managed to say. "I don't break laws willfully. No matter how big it was, I didn't see the sign. I was so anxious to reach my destination before dark."

"You're very lucky that you have an out-of-state license or I would have to arrest you!"

"Oh, dear," I said, tears coming to my eyes. I was really hurt. "That has never happened to me before. I thought everyone in this town was so friendly and kind and when you blinked your light, I was so happy. I thought you blinked a welcome; now I feel so let down."

"Pull over there, to that side of the road," he barked.

I pulled over, my hands shaking. It was dark and I felt so far away from home.

He got out of his cruiser and came up to my window. "What are you doing here?" he asked.

"I am the speaker for a religious retreat and I am afraid right now I am lost. It's too dark to find my way."

"What road is the camp on?"

I told him the name of the road.

"Follow me," he said, but now he was smiling. "I have an errand to do and then I will escort you to the road."

"Thank you," I said, feeling happy again. "I am an author. Would you accept one of my books for your kindness?"

He nodded and smiled more broadly.

I took a *Papa's Wife* from my trunk.

"It will give you many laughs," I said as I gave him the book. "My Mama seemed to get into unexpected trouble, too."

He got into his car and I followed and waited until he had completed his errand. Then he came walking toward my car accompanied by two ladies.

"These two ladies live next to the camp to which you are going," he informed me. "You just follow them and there is no chance of your getting lost."

I arrived safely at my destination. All had gone well after all.

No matter how far I travel or how exciting it is to meet new challenges and wonderful people, the most exciting time is returning home. It is good to work around the house and to get out into the yard, and I love to cook. How precious the dinner hour is when Bob and I can be together. Bob does not ask many questions, and he does not always say that he is glad to see me back; but I know he is. The most wonderful thing about married life which has matured through the years is that you don't need to be told things over and over again; you just know. At times we talk very little. We might sit in front of the fire in the living room reading or looking at television. But there is that deep sense of well-being which comes over us, a deep gratefulness for the knowledge that we have each other and that God has protected us while we were apart.

"Oh," I often say, "I am so happy to be home!"

Bob will laugh then. "And soon you will be off again, and the grin on your face says that you're never happier than when you're traveling."

That's true in a way, I think; I really am happy and lighthearted when I start off on a new trip. That is because I love my work and people and God's great big wonderful world. So Bob is probably right at that.

Sometimes people forget that I have a home and husband to think of, and they don't know how hard I work at being a housewife.

I remember once at the close of a club meeting where I had been the speaker I happened to say to a lady, "It's time to get going now; my husband will be waiting for his dinner."

I shall never forget the look on her face. She looked almost crushed. "Don't do that to me!" she cried. "You're not like the rest of us who have to cook and clean and wait on our family. I thought you were above all that."

"Not at all! I do all of that besides speaking and writing. I go home to set that table and get dinner ready and pick up the dishes."

I felt I had wronged her in admitting this, but it was true. Being an author and lecturer is such a small part of my life. If I had only that, I would be missing so much of what it means to be a woman. God created us to be very special to our families, even though it means lots of hard work at times.

Yes, before I start out on a speaking trip, I first have to see that my house is in order. There are always last-minute things, like seeing that there is plenty to eat in the refrigerator—meatballs, sliced ham, cheese, fruit—

things that are easily picked up if there is no one to serve them. Beds have to be made and the house has to be tidied up. Little notes have to be placed here and there; on my husband's bed—"Good night, dear, I'll be thinking of you!"; or on the kitchen table—"Don't forget to take your vitamins!"; or a special note on the mirror of Bob's bathroom—"I love you!" All those things take time, but they make such a difference when a man comes home at night to an empty house. It is worth the time over and over again. I call it leaving a little bit of me behind.

"How long will you keep up this speaking and driving?" friends may ask.

I have to reply, "I don't know; as long as the will to go is there and as long as I am in demand. If a speaker is busy, it shows she is liked and needed. My plans are enfolded in the great master plan of my earthlife. I have my certain little acre to work on for my God. And whatever I do on it must be done well, with love and zest and vigor. This is my life and I thrive on it. When you do something you love, it is not a hardship; instead I find new strength in it and new joy.

I have also learned many valuable lessons on my travels. Once I spoke in a town near Boston, Massachusetts, during Lent. I spoke on Faith. I thought it was a successful talk, but that night my own words were to bounce back to me. Over refreshments after the meeting, I got into a discussion with a lady about the Boston strangler. She told me many frightening things about her town and how near it was to the city; in fact, who knew, the strangler might even live in that town.

Now I should have known better. When you have faith in your heart, you slam the door quickly if fear wants to come in; but I forgot to shut my door. When I arrived at the home of my friend where I was to spend the night, I was almost sick with fear of that awful strangler. I had stayed in this house many times before and the couple who lived there had become very dear to me. It was an old house and for the first time I saw that the locks on the doors and windows were very insecure. I was given the downstairs bedroom while the couple slept upstairs. We talked a little before we retired. I told about the conversation I had had with the lady and admitted I was scared half to death.

"May I have a light on in the living room?" I asked, feeling like a child again.

"Of course." My friend laughed. "In the dining room too if you'd like one. It seems so strange; I just can't picture you being afraid like this."

I was ashamed of myself, but it did not lessen the fear.

"No, the living-room light will be enough," I assured her.

But after I was left alone downstairs, my fear seemed to increase. I was too frightened to go to sleep. I knelt to pray, but my words only reached the ceiling and then seemed to fall down again. I got into bed and reached into my pocketbook for something to read. I always put in some kind of reading material before I leave home. What I pulled out was a *Guideposts*, several years old. I opened it at random; reading would have to take my mind off myself.

My eyes fell on the open page. I stared at it for a moment. Then I read these words: "My Son, Now I Am Going to Talk to You About Fear."

I could hardly believe my eyes, but I began to read rapidly. It was the story of a father telling his son that at sometime in life, sooner or later, he would meet fear; and the father wanted to prepare him for it. It was a beautifully written article, exactly what my soul needed. It could just as well have been written for me. It ended in a very effective way.

On an old fireplace in England, someone had carved some words into the stone. No one knew who had written them nor why, but these were the words:

> Fear knocked at the door
> Faith opened it
> And there was no one there

I almost laughed aloud. All my fear blew away. God had known that this would happen and He had guided me to put that little magazine into my purse. He had spoken to me . . . as clearly as if I had heard His voice. Again I repeated the words to myself, and this time when I prayed, I was sure that my prayer was heard. I was safe, for wherever I was, God was. I soon went to sleep and slept until late the next morning.

~12

I am happy now, when I think back to my childhood,
that as a youngster I believed that every mountain had
its troll and that every deep, deep forest had its giant,
and that good and bad elves really did exist.

I can remember one summer morning when I awoke
early and tiptoed softly to my window to look out into
the magic wonder world of dawn. The sun was shining
on the flowers in the garden, making the dewdrops
glisten like diamonds. Far off in the distant woodland a
cuckoo bird was calling; and as I stood there looking, I
saw the little folk for the first time. Down by the lake,
in the soft green grass, some elves were dancing. They
were very, very tiny, but they were there and it made
the morning such a special one. I know now that my
imagination was at play, but no one could have con-
vinced me of it at the time. They were as real to me as
life itself. My mind, perhaps, was a little confused between this magic world which was such a wonderful
mystery and God's world which I knew so well. I knew
that God walked on earth, although I could not see
Him. I knew that He always saw everything I did and
that I had to be careful to do the right thing. I knew
that I had one particular angel which was mine alone,
given to me by God to watch over me always. Yes,

angels were real! My angel sat on my bedpost at night and spread its great white wings over me like a canopy. The angel remained there all night and I had nothing to fear as long as I was good.

But it was the elves that I played with and that walked with me up the mountain slopes. I could hear their little feet trotting beside me. What a wonderful world with angels and elves! I was a little mixed up about all this as a child, but as I grew older and realized that part of my world was strictly make-believe, I had to separate them and discard the imaginary. I was so happy then that God and His angels were real and that I could keep them forever in my heart. I was not sad when I had to let the others go because God was so great that He filled all the vacant space. I think reality becomes more real if one has been allowed, as a child, to live for a few years in the world of make-believe. That is why little children's eyes are so big and round and filled with sparkle, and the children's world can be especially enchanting at Christmas time.

I know that is why it was so easy for me to write *Once Upon a Christmas Time*. The memories of childhood's Christmases lived within my heart. I had more fun writing this book in the fall of 1964 than ever. I would never have needed to record this material for my own sake, but when I gave my Christmas talks about my native land, people were always looking for a book to go with it.

"Where is your book on Christmas in Sweden?" they would ask.

And that was what made me decide to write one and this little Christmas tale has found a warm welcome among the American people. I have been so thrilled with the way it was accepted.

People so often ask about my method of writing books. Do I write at certain times of the day or in a certain place? No, I write whenever I have a chance. I have a portable typewriter on a black TV tray and I move it around to wherever I feel like sitting. Most of the time I write in the living room in front of the big picture window. I watch the automobiles go by and the children pass on bicycles and sometimes a young mother walking with a baby in a carriage. It makes an interesting picture. There is only one place where I cannot write; I cannot write looking at a blank wall. I crave space and freedom. As a rule, when I sit down to work, I finish one whole chapter at a time. It is, of course, a rough draft, but I always feel that the first copy is the best. Many times, after I have rewritten it a second or third time, I will discard the later copies and use the first. But I almost always write two. As I have said so often both to people and in my books, I don't bother about the spelling or sentence structure. I leave that to my younger daughter, Carolyn, who still does all my correcting.

Carolyn is now Mrs. Charles Jackson Barstow and has her own home in Greenwich, Connecticut. She teaches high-school English and devotes her time to being a teacher, a housekeeper, and a sweet wife to her Jack. Their household has two magnificent cats—Herman and P.G.—black and silky with white markings. I hope someday I shall have some grandchildren there to visit. Cats are so soft and cuddly, but they cannot take the place of a cooing, dimpled baby.

Carolyn has a quiet, easy way about her, so like her father. She is very conscientious and she handles my manuscripts in the same manner. Very often I have to wait for them; her school work comes first and I know it should be that way. I am very fortunate having such a fine editor right in the family. Yes, Carolyn has become a part of my books.

Our older daughter, Shirley, now Mrs. Hugh Loveland, lives on Long Island with her four children. My grandchildren are growing up too fast. But how lucky and blessed we are to have four such nice ones. They are very close to us and love to visit us in Longmeadow. Robert is fourteen now; when this book comes out, he will be fifteen. He is tall and redheaded with dark brown eyes. Each child has his individual traits and each looks different from the others. Gary, who will be thirteen in 1966, is dark-haired with eyes which are almost black—the complete opposite of Richard, who is ten and has blond hair and blue eyes. Richard looks very much like his Grandfather Bjorn did when he was a boy. Then comes my only granddaughter, my pride and joy, who is a brunette with blue-gray eyes. I think she looks a little bit like me and that is the way it should be. Perhaps Deborah Lou will grow up to be a writer, too. Who knows?

Shirley is a lot like Mama was. She is always into fifty million things—forever busy with clubs, church, P.T.A., and cub scouts. To top it all off, she has gone back to college to pick up where she left off many years ago. Being a professor's wife with four youngsters to bring up should be enough, but her time seems to stretch like a rubber band, and there is always room for just a little more. Shirley has something of my disposition; she bubbles over with fun and excitement.

Both of my girls are very precious to my heart. It was not so very long ago that both of them played in our back yard and that I had to comfort them and kiss their bruises and little hurts. Life has a way of moving along and taking us with it. I don't know where the time has gone, but it is good when one can look back on happy memories.

My life is certainly a busy one. The days go too fast. I wonder now how I had time a couple of years ago to teach creative writing in Springfield's Adult Educational Program. That was one thing that I never had dreamt would come to me. As I, along with the other teachers, was sworn in, I wondered over the turn my life had taken. I did not have the required education to teach, but I was accepted for what I had accomplished in my writing. It was an evening course, running for a number of weeks at a time, and it gave me such joy to share some of the knowledge I had obtained from writing my books. I had wonderful students, and I found there was one talent I did have—the talent to inspire every student to dare to believe in himself. I lit the spark that ignited the fuse that fired each one of them to try harder than ever before to get his work published. We had many unforgettable evenings together. From this class I found, to my surprise, that teaching was a totally different thing from writing. Because I had never studied composition, I had to take the finished product apart to see what substance it contained. How hard I had to study to be able to put all those ingredients back together. I loved it, but it was very time consuming and a lot of bother. It was really hard work; and after a day of traveling, speaking, and teaching a class, I was deathly tired when the day was over. I had never met lovelier people though than those who attended my classes. They were of various ages and some of them were excellent prospective authors. I hope to read their names on books someday, and I pray that I may have a little bit to do with their success. After two terms I gave up teaching school. I felt that I was spreading myself over too many surfaces, and I needed time for my own writing and for my home. I know it was the right thing to do, but I was never sorry that I had tackled the task, even if just for a short while.

Once Upon a Christmas Time was my fifth book. I shall write at least eight—one for each child in the parsonage—of which this is my sixth. Just now I have nothing in mind for the future, but I know that after a little while, something will come to me and then it will be fun to start creating again. I have also written one article and many Sunday-school stories. In the thirties I wrote many short stories for Sunday-school papers. They were my first attempt at English. It all came about because of a Dr. Jones from Philadelphia, who asked my sister Margaret to write something for the Sunday-school paper of which he was editor. She laughed and told him that she was not an author.

"But we have one in the family," she said. "My oldest sister writes, but only in Swedish."

"Tell her to try to write in English and we will correct it," he urged.

And I did! The editors were wonderful to take my stories, correct them, and pay me for them; and I wrote quite a few stories, so that experience too belongs to my life. Knowing that I could do it enriched and thrilled me. I am forever grateful to Dr. Jones for accepting me when he had counted on my educated sister. Perhaps the confidence I gained in myself at that time had a lot to do with my final success.

How simple my life really is. I have no degrees and no official position, but I do have faith, self-confidence, and a desire to create. Out of this my books have been born. They have been thought out in the midst of cooking and doing dishes and planning meals. I have never claimed to be a great author, but I do claim to be a good one. I know that my books have gone into people's homes and established themselves there as a definite influence, helping families to change their way of living to fit the books. That is enough glory for me. It warms my heart. If one has a talent, I believe he can produce if he attempts it without fear; often one is greater than he thinks. If *I* could write, almost anyone could try it. People today seem to have so much more to work with than I had in the beginning. Yet I made it!

I have been so thrilled with the many letters that have reached me, the friends I have made, and the places to which I have traveled. I don't know how long I shall keep on, but as long as I feel well, as long as I have the desire to go, as long as people want me, I shall continue. When I get older, I shall sit down in a rocking chair and look back on life. I shall have time then to take out each memory, examine it, and relive the years when I was so busy. I would very much like to live until I am over ninety-five. I would like to see a new century march in. Perhaps I can live that long if it is God's will. Then I'd like to go to sleep, full of years and satisfied to leave earthlife. It would be like stepping out of an old dress and slipping into a new one. I want to look forward to death as Mama did. I wonder more and more now what eternity holds. It must be beautiful! It must be wonderful to close your eyes on earth one day and open them and see Heaven the next. The mind cannot grasp beyond that step, however.

A lifetime goes very quickly. I have told my story while I still plan on for many years ahead; yet it all rests in God's hands. And I am grateful for the years I have had, the good ones that have been so fruitful and even the lean years that were hard to endure. They were good for me, and I learned many valuable lessons. As I close this chapter, I am grateful that I can share so much with my readers, even though I have met so few of them personally. They are such a part of me, and they are my friends.

Here is a letter which proves this point:

Dear Mrs. Bjorn,

Although I have not met you, you are one of my closest friends. I feel that I know your whole family. I shall never feel lonesome again when there are people like you in the world who live and help and heal. God surely has given you a gift and a heart that can love and feel for others.

I have read your books over and over again, and each time they seem new to me. Please keep on writing and keep on sharing, and I have one request above all the others, please never change.

Your unknown friend,
Lois

It is letters like this one that made me write this book. I hope that it will make people feel even closer to me than before, because now I know I am more than an author to so many—I am truly and surely a friend.

⌐13

It is lots of fun to be the mother of daughters! I wouldn't have missed it for anything. Of course, once in a while some person will say, "Wouldn't you have liked to have a son?"

"Yes," I say truthfully, "Bob and I would have loved to have a son."

But then there is that wonderful part of life with daughters. If they marry, you acquire sons one day, and they can become as close to you as your very own. It is true that you don't always appreciate them when they first come on the scene, and our Jack had a very hard time getting into the family circle.

He was different from the other boys who had dated our younger daughter. To us he seemed too much a man of the world, and in the beginning she didn't seem too sold on his company, so Bob and I did not worry about it. He seemed older than his years, was widely traveled, and his manners were flawlessly charming.

And there was the father-daughter relationship that Jack was up against. Carolyn and her dad were the greatest of pals. Bob had no intention of taking a back seat and his actions demonstrated it clearly. It was embarrassing to me to discover that every time Jack came into our living room, Bob had an excuse to leave. It made me ill at ease in our friendly home to see Bob give Jack the cold shoulder. There was very little conversation between them, and the strain seemed to get worse as the weeks went by.

Then Carolyn and I decided to take a trip to Sweden in the summer of 1963. This was a gift to Carolyn from her father who was anxious for her to see the places where we both had been born and spent our childhoods and to meet those of our folks who were still alive. It would be a wonderful trip and we both looked forward to it.

But Jack took no chances. He had made up his mind to marry our daughter and now she seemed to put no obstacles in the way. Then we realized that she was in love with him!

"Mother," she said one night, "I am going to get an engagement ring from Jack before I go to Sweden."

"Oh, no, Carolyn!" I protested. "It would break your father's heart. I think he's secretly hoping you will meet a real Swede over there and get Jack off your mind. Can't you wait with the ring until we come back?"

"No, Jack is set on our being engaged before I go, and I've agreed; but I told him he'd have to get Dad's approval."

"Poor Jack!" I sighed. "If he goes to see your father, he'd better take with him all the courage he can muster."

"He'll find a way," Carolyn laughed.

And he did! I really was proud of Jack and a little awed, and I could visualize the whole scene so plainly after he told me how he managed to get on the right side of his future father-in-law. Bob was taken by surprise that afternoon when Jack walked into his shop. Perhaps he even was a little alarmed, wondering what had brought him there. But Jack got right to the point, as only he could.

"Mr. Bjorn," he began, "I'd like to take a few minutes of your time to talk to you man to man."

Bob half-smiled, giving Jack that X-ray look of his.

106

For a few seconds there was an awkward silence. Jack cleared his throat.

"I know, sir," said Jack, "that you realize that for a long time I have been very fond of your daughter. I would like to give her a ring and I'm asking your permission."

Bob did not answer right away. He stared at Jack who at that point looked a bit helpless, pleading, and very humble.

Then Bob spoke. "It is not the custom of our time for a young man to come to ask for a daughter's hand in marriage. I am rather surprised."

"I wasn't thinking of the custom of our time. I am very anxious to have your consent."

I can't help but think of how much it must have cost Jack to say that, after all the months of cold treatment he had received, no matter how hard he had tried to break down the barrier. And I am sure that at that moment Bob remembered another time, many years ago, when he had been a young man in love, who, not daring to go to his future father-in-law, had written him a note and then anxiously waited for the outcome. Could it have been those thoughts which suddenly changed his attitude? His coolness seemed to melt away as he reached out his hand to Jack.

"Well, there isn't much I can do about it when you put it like that. I do appreciate your coming to me, and I trust you will make Carolyn happy. That is all that matters. Go and buy the ring."

Jack hesitated a moment and then their hands met in a firm handshake.

"I have a confession to make," Jack said sheepishly. "I don't know what I would have done if you had refused." And he took a little box from his coat pocket. "You see, I already have the ring."

They both laughed wholeheartedly. All the gloom vanished and Jack had a chance to display that lovely little token that was to seal a courtship until the wedding day.

A few minutes after Jack had left Bob's shop, the

telephone rang in our home. Carolyn and I were sitting at the kitchen table having our afternoon coffee. I answered the phone and heard my husband's gay voice on the other end.

"You'd better kill the fatted calf," he jested. "There's going to be a wedding in our house very soon. Jack is coming over with a beautiful ring for Carolyn."

I could hardly believe my ears.

"How do you know?" I blurted out.

"Oh, Jack was here and we have settled the whole matter. He didn't want her to leave for Europe without a ring on her finger."

I turned to Carolyn after I hung up.

"It was your father," I said, "and Jack has done it. He did find a way. Your Dad is all excited about his future son-in-law. He says Jack is on his way over with your ring, and he was happy about it! It is a miracle!"

"There's always a miracle, Mother, when you're in love," she said.

And that was that. The ring was beautiful—a center diamond with a deep-blue sapphire on either side—so right for Carolyn. She wore the ring proudly and eagerly began to wait for February, 1964, when the wedding would take place. But there were still months of teaching and preparations, and before that, the long, beautiful summer—a summer which a mother and daughter would spend together relaxing and having fun. And the separation would be good for the engaged couple. There would never be a better way to test their love than putting a whole ocean between them.

I wish that every mother of a prospective bride could have been as lucky as I was—a whole six weeks of being alone together in the most favorable circumstances; what could be better? Shirley and Hugh, Bob and Jack were all there when Carolyn and I took off into the blue. I know the parting was hard for Carolyn. We had no more than unfastened our seat belts when she wished we were back home again. How impatient young love is.

108

And I thought that many times in Sweden as we traveled from place to place with Carolyn checking off each day on her calendar. But we had a wonderful time, and I know that Carolyn will never forget that summer. She fell in love with Stockholm because there were so many places to shop. She loves shopping. I get tired of stores easily, but when I could not go with her, she ventured out alone and in her halting Swedish, managed to buy whatever her heart desired. There were more and more bundles for that little home that soon would be. I let her shop while I busied myself with relations, friends, and dear old places. We spent some time with my husband's people, and Carolyn learned about the modern country life of Sweden and a lot of extra good cooking.

In Östergötland we took many trips to see much of the old, old Sweden. Castles were Carolyn's favorites and the old churches were mine. Among other places, we visited Vadstena where so much of the history of the Catholic Sweden is still in view. I loved the ruins of the cloisters and there was also an old castle which fascinated Carolyn and took much of her time.

Once I left her wandering about while I visited a place that held a special interest for me. It was a villa behind a high wall. I had been told that nine nuns lived there. I felt a desire to learn a little about what they were doing among the remains of the old cloisters that dated back to the year 1370. I wondered what mission the nuns could have in Sweden in 1963. And being me, I had to find out.

So I stood that lovely summer afternoon outside the heavy wooden gate on which was written: *The Saint Birgitta Order*. It was this wonderful saint who had built the cloister and the historical church in which her body was entombed. Were the nuns here to try to change the religion of the people? Oh, there were so many questions in my mind, as I pulled the large bell and waited.

In a few minutes the gate swung open and a young nun smiled at me.

"Welcome," she said in broken Swedish. "Come inside."

I explained to her the reason for my visit, that I was a tourist from America and because I was a speaker, I was very much interested in an interfaith program then trying to iron itself out in the world. Why were there Catholic nuns in Sweden? Why did they live in this beautiful Villa? Was it true that they were here to convert the Swedish people to their faith and try again to turn Sweden into a Catholic country?

That was a lot to say in one breath. But I wanted to make myself clear from the beginning.

"I think you would like to speak to Sister Maria. She is Swedish, the only one of us born in this country. I know you would like to talk in Swedish, so you would enjoy her the most. But just now all the other nuns are at Vespers. I am the only one here to tend the gate, but I'd love to show you around a little while we wait."

I looked at her habit, which was different from any I had ever seen. It was gray with a black veil. On the veil was a white linen crown with pieces of red cloth sewed on it, symbolizing the crown of thorns our Saviour wore, the red representing the five deep wounds. The dress of the order of Saint Birgitta of which these nuns were members was unusual and very impressive.

"This is a beautiful garden," I said, thinking to myself that the different flower beds, a mixture of every imaginable flower including red, pink, yellow, and white roses, could also be a symbol of all the different faiths, blooming together before the Lord in the garden of life.

"We tend the garden ourselves," the nun said. "We do all the work around here, both inside and out."

"It is so beautiful!" I exclaimed.

And it was breathtakingly beautiful. I felt as if I had suddenly been placed in another world filled only with joy, love, and peace. The nun guided me to a little chapel. It was very small, peaceful, and quiet. The stained-glass windows and the simple altar almost demanded that I remove my shoes in this holy place. In the distance I could hear the chanting of the hymns from the Vesper service and the low, even tones of the prayer said in unison. Presently, I felt an urge to pray, too, a feeling mixed with despair because of the great gulf that separated people even when they spoke the same language, worshiping the same Lord. I wanted to cry. I wanted to kneel. Oh, I wanted so much to be a little part of all this beauty, and not a stranger, not an intruder.

The sister took me by the arm and ushered me out into the long hall that led to a majestic dining room with large windows facing a wide blue lake. The furniture in this room was hand carved and ornamented with real gold. Heavy brocade draped the windows and covered the chair seats, all in gold and blue, all fashioned masterfully by the busy hands of nine nuns.

The library with many hundreds of volumes of beautifully bound books was our next stop and here the Swedish nun caught up with us. We faced each other smiling as she spoke to me in pure Swedish, explaining about their villa and why they lived here in such beauty and luxury.

"This is not a nunnery. It is a rest home," she informed me. "It is open to the public. Anyone can come and rent a room here to get away from the noisy, busy world for a while. This is our way of serving Our Lord. We do not speak of our faith, but we try to live it in every little detail, and only if we are asked, are we free to speak. People come here wounded by life and with their hearts broken. They have lost faith, and here we help them to find it again. We plant love and kindness and understanding in their souls, and they come back again and again. This is how faith is reborn and how we get most of our Swedish converts."

How well I understood. If I had not had a living faith, I too, would have wanted to know about theirs; I felt that I had learned much in this short hour and a great desire filled my soul to follow my Master more closely and more faithfully so that I could spread joy and sunshine about me as these nuns did.

Before we left the library, Sister Maria gave me a dozen little booklets concerning the Catholic faith and written in Swedish.

"This is so you will better understand us and our purpose in Sweden," she told me.

We shook hands and parted at the big gate, smiling at each other as it shut. I was back in the world. People around me were rushing and pushing and laughing and talking in loud voices. A cloud covered the sun and a cold wind blew from the lake. I longed to go back inside the gate. I was glad I had made the visit. I was grateful that the Birgitta nuns had opened a rest home in my Sweden. It was good that they were there . . . and so right. Somewhere deep, deep, within me there was a hurt. For an hour we had been close; now the great gulf separated us again.

"Why?" my heart cried. "Why?"

The cry has not yet been answered. I still don't understand so many things. But the Master's words come to my mind: "He that is not with me is against me; and he that gathereth not with me scattereth abroad."

Even after we returned to America and our lovely trip was but a memory, I enjoyed thinking back to that beautiful rest home by the blue lake in Sweden. There was a quietness and peace there that was different from any other place I had ever been. Some of it must have rubbed off on me because I felt it while Carolyn and I toured the northern part of Sweden.

While taking a side trip to Norway, we stopped in Lapland to visit Papa's little church, now abandoned, unused, and forgotten, looking up at the mountain that Papa and Mama used to climb. We climbed it too—by taxi most of the way. What a climb—but what a magnificent view from the top! It was almost like standing on top of the world, way up there above the Arctic Circle. We took tours on trains, boats, and planes. I was glad my daughter could see all this and that she could form her own opinion of the land where her parents were born and played as children. But no matter how much fun we had and how much beauty we had seen, Carolyn still longed for the day of departure and the journey home to Jack.

After another trip—to lovely, gay Copenhagen, Denmark (a city which Carolyn loved)—we took a Swedish-American ocean liner from Gothenburg to New York.

As we stood on the deck that summer day waiting the hour of departure, we observed the goings-on at the dock: people hustling and bustling about, and tears and laugher as loved ones parted. We watched the stewards carrying in load after load of flowers. We anticipated a joyous welcome in America, but here we had no one to say farewell to us.

"It's too bad we have no one to wish us a bon voyage or send us flowers," I said, clasping Carolyn's arm. "It's sort of sad that our friends are so far from here."

"I don't care," said Carolyn, laughing. "All I care about is getting started for home."

"And Jack . . ." I teased.

We stood on deck until we were quite far from land and then we went down to our cabin. As we opened the door, we both stopped. There on our table stood a beautiful bouquet of yellow roses.

"Who could have sent us roses?" we both asked at once.

There was a card. Carolyn reached it first and then smiled.

"They're from Jack, Mother! He sent me roses, wishing me a happy trip home with love. And look; there's one rose for each day of the trip. How sweet of him!"

"We did get flowers after all!" said I. "From someone way across the sea!"

I felt fine about Carolyn getting married. Love had been tested and it had been strong enough to last. The distance never even made a dent in it.

Later that summer our family was seated in our garden. There were still the three of us. This particular night Carolyn was waiting for Jack to take her out. It seemed that Bob and I treasured every minute we had with her now, realizing she would soon start a life of her own. This was late August and February first would come much too soon. There was a scent that filled the air from Bob's roses, and I remembered another garden and other roses. Carolyn seemed thoughtful too.

"A penny for your thoughts, dear," I said.

"Oh, Mother, I was back in Sweden again. I was thinking about that old, solemn, gray stone castle and I remembered the story of the knight who climbed that wall to the window of his princess. How much in love he must have been to dare."

"Yes," I continued, "and he was caught by the guards and imprisoned in a hole in the wall by her cruel brother. The hole was so shallow he couldn't stand up and there was no light at all."

"It was awful," interrupted my daughter, "and I'll never forget it. You remember that when they finally released him, he was blind."

"And he never got his princess, I presume," laughed Bob.

"That's right," said Carolyn. "What a price to pay for love!"

Jack came across the lawn, and Carolyn went to meet him.

The night grew dark and the garden was cool. Bob and I still sat there, both of us deep in thought. Then I told him about the nuns in Sweden and that wonderful garden.

"It was love that placed them there," I said thoughtfully. "There are so many different types of love. They also paid their price, giving their lives in a mission to help people find God and peace in a restless disbelieving age. The love they give will never die. It is a beautiful love."

I reached out my hand for Bob's. Soon we would be two again, as we were in the beginning. We paid our price for love, too. Letting one's children go is not

114

easy, but it is right. And we had had fun then, years ago, when we were only two. We would have fun again. This was all a part of life, and I made up my mind that I would do all I could to make the sunset of our lives really beautiful and I hoped we would have many long years together.

✤14

February, 1964, came upon us much too soon. There had been such busy months of preparation for the wedding, and January had been a very special month for the bride-to-be with luncheons and dinners and showers galore. She, of course, was busy teaching every day and Jack, who had a job in New York City, came to Longmeadow only on weekends. And there was always so much to show him, so many gifts that had been received. And then, of course, so many plans to be discussed and names to be added to the wedding-invitation list, which was already too long.

I presume that every mother is thrilled preparing for a wedding, and I was no exception. I loved the very thought of it, and I planned to make it the prettiest wedding that ever had been. I took all January off from my speaking and writing so I could devote all my time to the task ahead of me.

It was quite strange for me to be just a homebody and to have time for all those little housewifely things that I had been forced to give up when I became a career woman. But I wanted that month to be given completely to Carolyn's plans and, as I think back on those days, I am glad that I made that decision.

My daughter was an unusually calm bride-to-be. She went about her teaching as if she were going to stay there, not as if she were stepping out of it into a new life in a few weeks.

"How soon will you stop working?" I asked her one cold January morning as we were having breakfast.

Carolyn looked up at me. "Stop?" she asked. "What do you mean?"

"I mean that you're getting married the first of next month, or have you forgotten?"

She laughed happily. "No. I still remember, but I'm not planning to stop at all. I'm going to work until the day before the wedding and that afternoon I'll have my hair done."

Now it was my turn to stare at her.

"But there are a million things to be done, my dear, and getting married takes a lot of preparation."

"Mother," said Carolyn, "you know you'd be terribly unhappy if you couldn't have your finger in all of it, so you can handle it and you have Frances to help you."

I was thinking about her last words after she had driven off in her car. I did have Frances! What in the world would our household do without her? I wished that every housewife could have someone like our Frances. What a wonderful world it would be! Too bad there was only one of her, but how blessed I was that I had her for a helper.

She had been coming to us every week for several years. I can't remember just how things were before that. Frances is of Polish descent; she is as fresh as an ocean breeze and as gentle as a spring shower. There is always a happy smile on her face. If I happen to be a little down or leaning toward the blue side, it all disappears as soon as Frances opens the door. That's the kind of person she is. She is filled with good will for the whole world. She will do anything you ask of her, and more.

There was one time when I was lecturing quite a distance away and learned that unexpected company was coming. I knew I would have no time to cook and get things ready, so I called Frances long distance and asked her to buy a turkey and roast it for me. When I arrived home, the turkey was there roasted to perfection and even the gravy was done. And there along with the turkey was a couple of delicious apple pies. That's the way Frances is.

I have often said that if there were doctorates given for housework, Frances would be the first to be honored with one. I thank God for her daily; she has become almost like a sister to me. What a help she is even in talking over problems. When she leaves our home on a Friday afternoon, everything sparkles. I often brag that I have the cleanest house in the whole world, not on my own merit, but because of one who takes as much interest in it as if it were her own. I hope she will always be with us.

Of course I talked the wedding over with Frances and she was a great help to me. There was the problem of our dear grandchildren. Shirley and her husband and children would arrive the day before the wedding, as both she and Hugh were in the wedding party along with our only granddaughter who was to be the flower girl. But what would we do with the three lively boys? It would be hard to have them underfoot. But Frances solved it in a fine way.

"I will invite the boys to come to my house and stay overnight. In fact, they'd better bring their clothes along and stay until the wedding and Joe and I will bring them. You are all in the party, so they might as well sit with us if that will help you out."

It was a wonderful idea that worked out just perfectly and solved one big problem. It might seem like a minor thing to some people, but for a busy housewife in the midst of wedding preparations, it was a blessing to find a place where the grandsons could be happy and still close by.

Of course, I had to bake and cook for all my company. And suddenly as I thought of the out-of-town guests, I realized how many new friends I had

118

made since the books were published. They were not just people from the publishing company, but all those whom I had met through my books who had become dear friends to Bob and me. There was that wonderful couple at the Cape who so often invited us to their place by the ocean for a summer weekend. But perhaps our oldest friends included The Silent Lady from my book, *Mama's Way*. She had been as close as any friend could be and her husband and Bob are pals. The four of us gather at our home mostly in the summer when Boston is so hot. They have a room ready for me any time I need to stay overnight around Boston. It has a big sign on the door which made me smile when I saw it. It is painted in brilliant colors and reads: "Button's Room." How lucky I am to have friends like that.

And then there are our friends in Brockton, close to us both. My friend's husband, an educator, had been peeved at his wife the first time she had invited me to stay at their home. He thought that because I was an author, I was a celebrity and that their entertaining me would not be good enough. The first time I spoke in their church, I stayed on a couple of days and we became good friends. He was glad then that I had come, finding me quite a simple, ordinary person. Bob enjoyed them too.

Then there was a couple near Hartford, Connecticut, with whom we became acquainted quite by accident. I shall never forget that night I spoke in a certain church in their vicinity. When I had finished, a gentleman came up to greet me.

"I have pictures at home on my slides of that mountain your Papa climbed," he said. "I come from Lapland, too."

We had a long talk, and he took down my address. Then a few weeks later on a Sunday night when Bob and I were just about to have a snack in our garden, a car parked in our driveway and a couple came into our yard. I recognized the man from Lapland. They joined us and invited us to see their slides. We did call on them, just at strawberry season, and they had strawberries growing in their yard. We had a feast, saw the slides, and formed a strong friendship. This wonderful man died a couple of years ago, and with him went so much fun and frolic. He was always the life of the party, but his wife is still just as close to us.

Oh, there were so many more wonderful people that had never met my Bob, but whom I considered my close friends. I could think of them all over the United States and in Sweden, Austria, and Peru. How I wished they all could have come to the wedding. Perhaps I had never realized before how many new friends my books had brought me. Carolyn's wedding brought them to mind in a fascinating way. I was grateful for those who could attend so that the new friends could meet our old ones. How very precious our friends are to us; they are surely a wonderful gift from God.

There were some members of our own family who could not come. The distance was an obstacle. My dear brother Nels had an important speaking engagement miles and miles away, and it could not be canceled; so he was missing. But, to our joy, his darling wife Katharine came. I remembered something she had said years ago when I was preparing for the first wedding in our household—something I never forgot. There had been so many details to take care of then and I wanted everything to be just so. At the last minute I was rushing around confused and tired and a little irritated.

"Oh, Katharine," I had cried out, "I don't know how to get it all done. I want this to be such a beautiful wedding."

Katharine had put her arm around me and smiled her calm, lovely smile.

"Thyra," she had said, "one of the most beautiful things at a wedding is the bride's mother—serene, calm, and collected."

Now, almost fourteen years later, I tried to remember that. In the rush of these days before the wedding, I told myself over and over again, "If this is going to be a beautiful wedding, I must not be too tired or irritated or confused." And it really helped.

But what a day it turned out to be! You would not have wished it upon your worst enemy. It sleeted and snowed with rain and fog mixed in to create a dreary darkness. But it did not dampen the fun and happiness in our household. In spite of the bad weather, many people who had traveled long distances arrived safely, and so did the members of the family. There was my sister Margaret who drove all the way from Philadelphia, all flushed and excited. Sister Ann from Cleveland and brother Folke and his wife Elaine from Rochester, New York, had arrived the day before. Folke was to perform the ceremony, assisted by our own pastor and Jack's Episcopal priest. Three ministers should do a good job of marrying our youngsters.

That morning while Carolyn went to the dentist, we all pitched in to decorate the reception hall, which was breath-takingly beautiful with flowers and silver and pastel tablecloths for all the small round tables for the guests. The long table in the center of the room required most of our attention. It was on that table that the dishes for the smorgåsbord would be placed. There were lovely, tall, silver candelabra and large brandy snifters with bouquets of soft pink and white carnations cascading down over the lace tablecloth. The room certainly looked like a wedding with ferns, palms, and floor-size candelabra standing by the bridal table, which was covered with white linen and blue lace. How fast the time went, and soon the capable hands of the caterer took over and we hurried home where all the bridesmaids were gathered.

The rooms seemed full of large white boxes and chatter and excited laughter. The groom's mother arrived dressed in peacock-blue crepe. Bob was fussing in his room, putting on his morning coat, which he had sworn he would not wear. He didn't like all the fancy clothes. But I had carefully said nothing with the result that he was now meekly putting it all on. The dress suit had been Jack's choice, although a tuxedo would have been punishment enough for the bride's father. But I

121

knew all the time that he would capitulate. Now the victory had been won. Carolyn was thrilled, although she would have accepted whatever her dad put on, loving him just as he was. But now everything was all right there and I could relax about that.

Our Debby looked as cute as a button and so excited that she had been included on this great occasion.

Finally, I began to dress too, putting on my long forest-green chiffon. It was very festive, and I felt calm and collected. Katharine would be proud of me.

Everyone seemed to be helping the bride. I really would have liked to do it all by myself—touching all those beautiful white, white things—but I let them be. Only when it came to the little gold bridal crown we had ordered from Sweden did I insist. After all, who knew more about wedding crowns from Sweden than I? Barbara, Carolyn's friend since schooldays, nodded her approval.

The photographer arrived and we found ourselves ready in plenty of time. Carolyn made such a beautiful bride that it almost made me cry. I couldn't take my eyes off her. And Shirley, too, could have taken a prize with little Debby close beside her. What lovely daughters God had given to Bob and me. But they were ours only for a few short years; then when they had grown up, you gave them away on a lovely occasion like this to someone else for a lifetime.

It was a candlelight service at dusk, although the weather made it seem even darker. The church was crowded with happy people. How beautiful it was. The flower arrangements and the candelabra with tall, white candles, the large stained-glass windows and the thick burgundy carpeting were part of the picture. By the altar stood the prayer bench, draped in heavy white satin.

Just at the right moment the long march up the church aisle began. Those lovely, lovely girls, dressed in soft burgundy velvet and satin with small burgundy pillbox hats, carried their pink and white bouquets so gracefully as the organ played. There was so much beauty and happiness everywhere. And then she came, the bride, my baby, walking slowly and lightly with her small hand on her father's arm. How handsome my Bob looked. The years had not seemed to change him. He was really giving his girl away to Jack. Her pink roses and white lilies were held against the white peau de soi gown and the sheer finger-tip veil was held by the tiny gold bridal crown.

There were stars in Carolyn's eyes as she came nearer and nearer to where Jack stood waiting. And so, Folke began the ceremony.

My heart skipped a beat when he asked, "Who giveth this woman to be married to this man?" Perhaps, I thought suddenly, Bob would change his mind and say, "No one does!" But he didn't! His voice rang out loud and clear, "Her mother and I do."

I didn't cry. The whole time I did not cry. It was all so right, so very, very right.

Shirley, too, looked beautiful and there was a smile on her face. No one would believe that she was the mother of four and the oldest a teenager. The years had dealt kindly with her; she looked as young as her sister, and I knew that in her heart there was a prayer that only happiness would come Jack and Carolyn's way.

Jack and Carolyn were now man and wife. And I prayed, "Dear God, keep them free from heartbreaks. Shower them with earthly happiness, but don't let them forget that true happiness comes only when they seek Thy kingdom first."

Yes, it was a perfect wedding! And the reception was as nice as it could be. There we all stood in the receiving line, greeting the people. How many there were, even on such an awful day. How wonderful they were to come and celebrate with us. And now I had time to give a bit of myself to those grandsons so dressed up and polite, sitting at the family table.

You can't help but feel good when everything has gone perfectly. Then there was the newlyweds' last visit to the house to dress for their trip. People drifted in and out to look at the beautiful gifts. The good-byes were not too painful. The bride and groom looked rather elegant going off together to Bermuda.

"We're leaving, Mother," Carolyn said.

I kissed her good-bye tenderly, wordlessly wishing her happiness from my heart, giving her only a tight squeeze and a hug. Jack, too, gave me a hug and a kiss. My big, new son would take good care of our girl. Bob shook hands with Jack and kissed Carolyn as casually as if she were just going for a ride. And then they were off.

That first night was so busy, with guests and coffee and food and laughter and fun that I did not have time to think much until all the company had gone home or to bed, and Bob and I were alone. It felt good to get into bed and to talk everything over. It had been a big day and I was very tired, as was Bob, who was soon asleep. *And just then it hit me.* I let the tears come. I was just a mother feeling sorry for herself. There was no more need to be calm and collected. It was all over and my little girl was gone—gone for good this time.

Bob slept soundly. I wondered about a father's heart then. How could he sleep like that? Wasn't a chapter of life ended? It would never be the same again. The house would be still; all the youth that had bustled around it would never come back. Carolyn had been such a wonderful daughter; she had given us so much joy. Presently, I wished that I could move the years back, that I could have her small again. I wanted to feel her chubby little arms around my neck and those wet kisses and those bear hugs. "Why do they have to grow up?" my heart cried. "Why does life go with such speed? Oh, just to have her little once more. To tuck her into bed and to hear her say her prayers, to have her back again even now . . ." I suppose all mothers go through that agony. And they love to suffer just this once; it goes with mother love.

I finally fell asleep and in the morning I was myself again, busy with food and company and, of course, talk of the wedding. But in my heart I couldn't help wondering if Carolyn missed us—if in all her happiness, she had just once thought of us. I had a strange feeling that perhaps when Jack was asleep, she had given over to the luxury of letting a tear roll down her cheek. To my heart, it seemed that this would make all things right.

∾15

Very often someone will ask me, "Are all you eight
parsonage children still living?"

I used to smile happily. Of course we were alive and
busy and well. We were the children of Papa and
Mama. It was the most natural thing in the world for us
to be alive.

Then came the fall of 1965. It started out so beautifully. It was as though the weather was trying to make
up for the hot, dry summer. The sun was warm as it
shone down on the earth, mingling its rays with trees
that were dressed in their coats of many colors. All was
well with our large family, and we were all excited
about our sister Margaret's new house. After her return
from a trip to Sweden and Germany that summer, she
found that an apartment house had been built just a
handshake from her living quarters. It annoyed her, for
now all she could see from her living-room window
was a gray wall.

She came to Longmeadow to visit us on Labor Day
weekend. I can still see her face as she came in at the
door, beaming with delight.

"You know," she said, "that apartment block they
built next to me has proved to be a blessing. I might be

126

crazy after spending so much money last summer, but I have just become the owner of my own home!"

"You mean to say you bought a *house?*" I said doubtfully.

"Yes, my dear, and it's the nicest house you've ever seen and just right for me." She began to describe it and there was no end to her flow of words. "It is in the town of King of Prussia, Pennsylvania, on a lovely street with a view, plenty of land, and all the rooms on one floor. The best thing is that now Gretchen has a place to run around."

Gretchen was Margaret's dog, a beautiful tan and black German shepherd, that was just as much a part of my sister as her arm or her leg. It was because of Gretchen that she had moved so quickly in the purchase of her new home. Since the apartment block had sprung up, there had been no place for Gretchen to be tied, no place for her to run.

"Someday I'll fence in the yard and then Gretchen can run free. This place is ideal—and it has three bedrooms!"

"Three bedrooms!" I cried. "Why does a girl with only a dog for her family need three bedrooms?"

I shall never forget the way she came over to me or the smile that was such a part of her. She hugged me tightly and placed her cheek against mine.

"Listen! I have seven brothers and sisters for a family! My dream has always been to be able to put all of you up for the night if you should come to visit at the same time. Oh, don't look so surprised. It could happen! And there are Thanksgiving and Christmas. I'll always want some of my family with me on the holidays. You and Bob are invited for my first Christmas."

We sat down in the living room to talk some more.

"My home will be as beautiful as yours, and I'm buying all new furniture. Just wait and see what I have picked out!"

I had never seen her so excited and happy. During her entire visit she talked continuously about her new home and her plans for the future.

"I want Bob to see the house soon," she continued. "A man knows a house, and I know he will admit this is a prize package." She smiled. "I got the loan without any trouble. It has all gone so smoothly as though every detail had already been planned for me."

"I'm so glad for you," I told her. "I think I'm happier for you than I've ever been for anyone else. You deserve it after all those years of hard work, getting along on a shoestring. I hope all the happiness in the world will come to you."

"I am happy, really happy! God has been good to me."

After the weekend had passed, I stood by her little Falcon as she prepared to start off for home. That was another thing about which she was proud and happy, her car. It had taken her years to afford such a luxury, but the few years she had had it, she had driven all over the United States. Her car was her friend.

She smiled as she started up the motor. I stood there waving as she backed out of the driveway and drove off. My heart was full of joy for her.

She is a wonderful sister, I told myself. How rich I am! I had said to the family on many occasions: "Let's include Margaret in all we do. We are her only family, you know."

"We always do include her, Mother," said Carolyn.

"Yes, but from now on she must be very special!"

I meant it. I never wanted Margaret to feel lonely or left out just because she wasn't married.

As I walked around attending to my household duties that morning, I was thinking of how much my sister had achieved. She had reached the height of her career. She had graduated from college in 1936. She had worked herself through without any help from home. Doing housework had not been easy and had taken much responsibility and her school work weighed heavily on her. Sometimes it had been 3:00 a.m. before she went to bed, only to arise again at the crack of dawn. There seemed to be so little time for her to study. But she made it with flying colors, and there had never been a happier girl. She became a high-school teacher and enjoyed her work for many years, but within her there was always that thirst for more knowledge; yet it took her ten years to take the step to attain it.

In 1946 she entered Eastern Baptist Theological School in Philadelphia as a student of religious education. Again she put everything she had into it and in 1948 she was appointed part-time instructor in German for the pre-theological division of the seminary. Her eyes were shining with delight. Now she was really getting somewhere. The German language had always held a certain lure for her and that was what she began to build her life around as she pushed on and received her Master of Religious Education degree from the seminary in 1949.

I wondered so often why she did not relax now. She could get a good-paying job and take life easy. But she had to do what her heart told her, and she plunged in to study even harder for her Master of Arts degree from the University of Pennsylvania, and two years later she was appointed an instructor of languages at Eastern Baptist College in St. Davids, Pennsylvania. It was a small college, but Margaret saw beyond the years and she did not mind the small salary. She knew that one day it would be different.

I scolded her at times. "For goodness' sake, Margaret," I would say, "you can do so much better in a secular college. You need more money now. You should have a little more time to enjoy life."

But nothing could change her mind. She loved her school. This was her college! It had a special mission and this is where she wanted to devote her time.

"Money is not what I am after," she assured me. "I think you should know that by now. The world needs a college like the one I'm serving. We don't give the students just book knowledge, but every day we carefully weave into their lives thoughts of God and the Christian life. I am grateful for each student who enters here. It is a real challenge and responsibility to teach them. To see young lives shaped into greatness of mind and soul is more valuable than money. I must work toward a higher degree so that I can give them even more. You see, I believe in the future of my college."

In 1962 she received her Doctorate of Philosophy of German Literature from the University of Pennsylvania. It almost broke her. She had had a lot of illness and her salary was small, but she threw herself into her studies with every fiber of her body. She studied late into the nights and in every available daytime moment. She lived in three small rooms over a beauty parlor and Chinese laundry. But it did not matter where Margaret lived; her home was her castle and she converted it into a lovely, cozy place. How she painted and decorated to make it attractive! The door to her home was always open to her friends and there was always a warm welcome for each one who entered. The memory of the days when I frequently visited my sister was doubly precious that morning as I was reminiscing.

Receiving her doctorate had not been all glory. Sickness had come upon her suddenly and unexpectedly just weeks before. She had landed in the hospital with cancer of the breast. But she had faced it unflinchingly, and God had granted her health once more. After that serious operation she had been out of the hospital only a week when she walked up the aisle in her cap and gown to receive her long-sought-after reward. Part of the family was with her and nothing could have made her happier than to share this moment with them. We were the joy of her life. And that same year, she was appointed full professor at the college and the plaque on her door read: *Dr. Margaret Ferré.*

The year 1965 saw her appointed Head of the Foreign Language Department. That was her last appointment from the college she had loved so dearly, the final step in reaching her dream. She had made it! She was satisfied. Her salary was large now; she received the maximum the college could give her—a reward for her eighteen years of service.

130

I can hear her shouting with joy: "I did what I set out to do! I made it! I have reached my goal!"

A trip back to Sweden had been a dream from the time she was a little girl. She still remembered so many things: the schoolhouse which she had attended, the dear old parsonage in which she had been born, the woods where she had played. She wanted to see all those places again. Then she wanted to visit the historical sites of Germany about which she was teaching her students. She wanted to walk where so many great men had walked, see their homes, and visit the museums. She wanted to mingle with the people and speak to them in their own tongue; all this would make her even a better teacher.

And she had that wonderful trip. Her heart was almost bursting with joy and excitement. She rented a small car and toured wherever she wanted to go. The ocean trip was a dream come true. She had such a wonderful time and made so many new friends. She returned filled to the brim with talk. She had been back only a couple of weeks when she bought her home and she was now moving into it.

"I can't afford to be sick this fall," she had said when I talked to her on the phone in her new home. "Whatever happens, I can't be sick!"

Was that why she did the impossible? Did she have a premonition? Her determination made her drive to the college and teach even when her body cried out for rest. She blamed it all on moving.

"It was too much for me," she said. "I've done more than I should. That's why I am so weak."

The men came and laid her beautiful new carpeting —a soft green to go with her gold drapes and walls. Slowly the new furniture came. What a beautiful home she was going to have! I often wondered if her heart told her what she refused to acknowledge? I have often wondered if, when she first had that dreadful backache, she suspected that the dreaded disease had returned to kill and destroy? Or did she close her mind to it be-

131

cause she wanted so much to live in her little home? I shall never know.

One beautiful fall Sunday Bob and I took one of our long walks. The first part of October can be so lovely. We walked briskly, our feet crushing the dead leaves that had blown into small heaps on the sidewalk. It seemed the world was too beautiful that afternoon to leave room for unrest, but something deep within me kept disturbing me, as though a soundless voice spoke to me in a way I knew so well. Whenever I felt that way, something was very wrong with one of my loved ones. How clearly that inner voice spoke to me. "Call Margaret," it said over and over until I could keep quiet no longer.

"Bob," I said, "let's turn back home. I have to call Margaret."

"Did you promise to call her this afternoon?" he asked.

"No, but I have that feeling again. Something is wrong with her! But it could be my imagination, of course. It might be just foolishness. . . ."

But Bob turned around. "No, I think you should call her," he said. "Even if all is well, it's better for you to call than to worry about it."

We walked quickly toward home. It was almost as though I wanted to run, it seemed so urgent. The afternoon had lost its beauty. There was an omen, something dark and strange and unreal. I got my sister on the telephone, but at first I didn't know her voice; it was so weak.

"What's the trouble, dear? Are you ill?"

"Yes, I am very, very sick. I've been fighting it, but I have such an ache in my back that I can't stand it. I can't keep food down and my mouth is as dry as a bone. I can't even take Gretchen out for a walk. I'm done for."

"Have you got any help?"

"A woman is here." She sighed deeply. "Don't worry; I'll be all right in a couple of days . . . I have to be."

132

"I'll call you again tomorrow."

"Thanks. I'm so glad you're coming for Christmas! I'll have lights inside and out. It will be so beautiful. Tell Bob not to back out."

"Oh, we're both looking forward to it. Just get well, dear."

She was too weak to talk any longer.

I called her every day that week, but she seemed worse each time, and on Saturday she was taken to the hospital. On Sunday afternoon, when I returned from a lecture, Bob told me the terrible news. Margaret had cancer of the spine; there was no cure for her.

I refused to believe it at first. "Oh, dear God, no!" I cried. "She must get well. She has just reached her goal. She can't stop living now!"

But her time was up. All her earthly dreams had come true, and now she was to graduate to the eternal world. One by one her brothers and sisters came to her bedside. Our doctor brother flew up from Miami, but there was nothing he could do to help. The illness showed on her dear face, but her smile was still there, wide and sweet as ever. There were no tears, no complaints, no regrets. We all prayed now—a strange prayer—that God would take her quickly. There were prayers everywhere. Faculty, students, friends, family, we all prayed one big prayer: "God take her quickly!"

The last day of her earthlife she became restless, just as Mama had. She couldn't wait! Once she reached out her hand as though she saw death coming toward her.

"Come," she said smilingly. "Come, let's go! I'm ready! What are we waiting for?"

"Where are you going?" my sister Ann asked tenderly.

Margaret looked up at her impatiently. "I am going to my Heavenly Father! Don't you know that?"

She prayed one last prayer when I was standing beside her. She folded her hands and closed her eyes.

"Dear God," she prayed, "I thank you even for this that has happened to me, but please, dear Lord, take care of Gretchen."

The call came in the night. The telephone rang out sharply in the darkness of her little home where part of the family slept. Margaret had gone in her sleep. She had stepped out of her earthly garment, and her soul had taken wings to another world where there was no sorrow or illness. How well God had answered our prayers. She had been in the hospital only one week.

There was a beautiful memorial service at the college; there must have been five hundred people there, paying tribute to Margaret. It was a lovely service with the college choir singing and some of her students singing in German, "A Mighty Fortress Is Our God." There were so many tributes of praise to her. And the family filled a whole row, the family sitting there deeply grieved by their loss.

But she really belonged here, I was thinking, with all these wonderful people and to this college to which she had devoted her life.

Outside the sun was shining on the beautiful campus. The red-tinted trees were mirrored in the small lake by the water wheel. How she had loved all this beauty! My heart ached and tears ran down my cheeks. How much I loved her and how I would miss her, as would the many others sitting there that day.

We put her to rest in the cemetery in Springfield, Massachusetts, where just a few years before she had stood with the rest of us by Mama's grave. Her friends were gathered there; she had so many friends. She was so rich!

The house was empty after they all had left. We were only seven now; it was the first break in the circle of children. My youngest sister Karin stayed on for a few days. It was good to have her; we could comfort each other. Perhaps we felt more than ever how precious a family is and how closely knit it can become. When one leaves, it is such a lonely, empty space. No one can ever fill it. Why did she have to go? We wondered.

But we must think of her with happy thoughts. She

was the *Greta* in my books, happy, jolly *Greta*, so lovable and full of fun. Now I must think of her as sailing away on another journey even though my eyes couldn't see the ship which was going on to the fairer land.

She had loved being a part of my books; and when I started this one, she was here so happy and alive. I did not know I would end it with the story of her death. She was so much a part of my life—a life given by God as a loan—one day to be given back to Him.

Now I must live my life so much more effectively because of her memory. I promised myself that it would be my tribute to my darling sister.

❧16

What strange turns life can take! We know nothing at all about what the morrow can bring. Bob and I had no idea that we were about to adopt a new member into our family. It was sudden, but it worked out just the same as putting a picture puzzle together. Without any effort, everything seems to fit into our pattern of life. Carolyn left such a big empty space in our home when she married and moved away. It had been such fun to be the three of us. And now we were going to be three again. What excitement there was in our household as the day of her arrival drew near. We were to meet her at the Bradley Field airport at 3:10 on a beautiful October Saturday afternoon. She was coming on a plane from Philadelphia. I can't remember having been so excited in a long time. I just hoped everything would work out and that she would like us and that we would like her. You take such a chance when you don't know.

About a week before, when my sister Karin was still with me, I had made a telephone call and today's arrival was the result of it. I could not get the thought of Margaret's dog out of my mind. The prayer that she had prayed echoed in my heart day and night. What had happened to Gretchen? If they had found a home for her, would the people be good to her? She was used to so much love. And if she was still in the kennel, how lonely she must feel. She would be waiting, I supposed, waiting for her lovely mistress to return as she had always done before. How long can a dog wait?

I knew nothing at all about dogs. As a child I had always been frightened of them. We had never had a dog when I was growing up. Papa and Mama had too many children to feed. But a dog must wait and listen, I presumed, listen for those well-known steps and for that voice to speak her name. What went on in a dog's mind anyway? The last I remembered of her was when my brother Folke and I took her to the kennel and said good-bye to her.

"Try to find a good home for her," my brother said, "and if there is no home, I guess you'll have to put her to sleep."

We had looked at each other. There was something glistening in Folke's eyes. I bent down and put my arms around her. She looked so sad and lonely.

"Good-bye, Gretchen," I said. "Be a good girl. We're sorry to leave you, but someone will give you a nice home."

She wagged her tail a little, but her soft brown eyes had a world of sorrow in them as though they wanted to say, "What has happened to me? I was the luckiest of dogs and had the most wonderful mistress, who adored me and gave me a warm, cozy home. Now suddenly she has gone away and everything is strange."

I cried a little. "Poor Gretchen," I said.

"It's so hard to leave her," said Folke.

An attendant came and took her away, and we drove back to Margaret's empty home.

A couple of weeks had passed since then. As a family, we had talked about Gretchen's plight, but each one of us was very busy and no one was able to take her. Yet she was almost like one of us. She had been so dear to our sister.

Karin and I had just had our coffee the morning I

137

called the kennel. I had said nothing about it to her, just put in the telephone call. I learned that Gretchen was still there. No, they had not found a home for her. She was fine, but a little lonely and confused.

"Could you arrange to have her shipped up to Longmeadow, Massachusetts?" I asked the veterinarian on the other end of the phone.

Of course they could. They would be glad to take care of every detail if that meant that we would take her and give her a home.

"That is my plan," I said. "Have her come next Saturday, and let us know what time to meet her. It will only take an hour from Philadelphia."

When I looked up, Karin was standing beside me and the tears were rolling down her cheeks.

"Thyra," she said, "you are going to give Margaret's Gretchen a home. That is the dearest thing you've ever done."

We cried in each other's arms.

"I might regret this all my life," I said, "but I had that dreadful feeling inside me that we were letting Margaret down. She loved Gretchen as much as she loved us."

"Oh, you'll never regret it. You'll never be sorry," Karin assured me. "I've never been happier over anything in all my life."

I called Bob and told him what I had done.

"It might work out fine," he said. "Perhaps we'll like having a dog."

And that night when Bob came home, he had bought a big, fancy bowl for Gretchen to eat from. The next day I did my buying: a bright-red leather collar, a leash, a twenty-five-foot chain for the back yard and something to anchor it to. And then I bought dog food. I tried to pick what I thought a dog would like, and ended up with several different kinds of food. After a while, I would know which food she liked best.

"She's not going to be a cellar or a kitchen dog," I told Bob. "She's used to sleeping in the bedroom and I want her to have the freedom of the house."

"That's quite a concession from a fussy housekeeper." My husband laughed, knowing very well that already I was worried about having dog hairs over everything.

"I don't care," I said, as though I wanted to convince myself. "I want Gretchen to be happy . . ."

I put an old coat of Margaret's in the back of Bob's station wagon when we left for the airport, hoping that it would make Gretchen feel that we were no strangers.

The plane was on time and, when all the passengers had departed, they had begun to unload the freight. There it was—a great big box with a screen on one side and something wiggling inside. It was Gretchen, all right! Oh, how big she was! I had almost forgotten that she weighed about one hundred pounds. She looked terribly unhappy in that cage—so bewildered and forlorn, and so anxious to get out. We talked to her, calling her by name. But when they took her out of her cage, she gave a quick jerk and broke the leash. What a time we had before we finally caught her and got her into the car!

I put the coat next to her. "We're going to be good to you. Please be happy," I pleaded.

Gretchen sniffed the coat and then licked it. She put her head on it and seemed to calm down, as we started our drive home.

When we arrived, she ran from room to room, sniffing and looking. She was still frightened, but I put my arms around her and patted her. "Welcome home!" I said with a big lump in my throat. "A big, warm welcome home, Gretchen!"

We let her sleep in the bedroom that night, and she seemed happy and content, but she disturbed us early on Sunday morning, wanting me to take her out. Of course, I did! And that was the first morning I walked with her at 6:00 a.m. She has kept that vigil ever since. Six o'clock is just Gretchen's morning hour, that's all. We soon realized what a beautiful dog she is. Her shiny fur was tan with black markings, her ears stood straight into the air, and her big tail wagged as though she wanted to let us know that she was grateful.

We had a hard time that first week because we could not keep Gretchen tied. She is a very strong dog, and she broke every collar and even the choke chain that was supposed to be fool proof. We were afraid to let her run loose. In the first place, she had never done it; and in the second, she was so big that she could easily knock over a child on his bike, and then we would be in a fine fix.

"I don't know what to do with her," I said to Bob one night. "She's such a lovable dog, but this breaking loose can't keep on."

"We might not be able to keep her," Bob said firmly. "We might as well prepare ourselves for the worst. But at least you know that we did the very best we could for her."

"You mean . . ." I said not even wanting to speak the words.

"Well, having her put to sleep won't hurt her. They do those things so kindly now."

I looked at Gretchen where she lay stretched out on the living-room floor. How silly she was not to behave when we could give her such a good home for the rest of her life. Already I loved her. There must be a way. There was always a way when one wanted something very badly. My mind began to work, trying to think just what to do to keep her in the yard. Then suddenly it was clear to me! Why hadn't I thought of it before? There was a perfect, secure way, if only Bob was willing.

"I think I know what to do," I ventured, weighing my words carefully. "We could fence in the back part of our yard, that extra land we bought a couple of years ago."

"A good idea," said Bob, "but a fence like that would be very expensive. And I'll bet she can jump. It would have to be at least five feet high."

"Let's think about it anyway," I suggested.

The very next day I had men at the house to give me

estimates on a fence. I hoped to get a good deal. It would be so wonderful both for her and for us if we could have that fence.

It was funny how I had bought that land in the first place. Bob had been dead set against it. He felt we already had too much lawn to take care of.

"Why do you want it?" he had asked me.

"Oh, I don't know, but there's something about a piece of land, Bob, especially land that is sold because it isn't wanted. It's as though it cries out and asks for a chance to prove itself."

He had laughed, saying, "You certainly have some ideas in that head of yours."

I felt hurt. "It's nothing to laugh at. I think all of us who come from the northern part of Europe feel like that; and you, who come from a home with plenty of farmland, should know what I mean."

"Well, I don't care. If you want that piece of land, go ahead and buy it, although I don't know what you'll ever use it for."

But now we knew. It was destined. It had all been planned ahead of time. It would be Gretchen's land.

We had had that land cleaned up and had bought loam for it and seeded it and last summer a silky green grass had covered it. We had even put a low wooden fence around it.

"There is something about a fence around your land," I had philosophized at the time, "that makes you feel that it really belongs to you."

Bob had looked at me as though he was trying to figure me out. To him, I always seemed to be saying strange things. But most of the time I had my own way.

Of course, we built Gretchen a strong, five-foot, chain-link fence. The men went to work on it right away; they gave us a good price and did a fine job. Before Thanksgiving Gretchen moved into her new quarters, and I've never seen a happier dog. She has three hundred feet in which to run free. And does she run! Sometimes you can only see a streak as we urge her on: "Faster, Gretchen! Faster! Faster!"

And now Bob is building a doghouse for her for her first Christmas present. It is insulated and will be the finest doghouse ever built. He is even putting in wall-to-wall carpeting, so she will be warm and snug when she needs a shelter. It is just big enough for her, and needs only a couple of coats of paint before it is placed inside her fence. What a lucky dog she is!

But we are luckier, because Miss Gretchen has stolen our hearts. She has brought something new and wonderful into our lives, something rare and precious. We have so much fun walking her. The nicest time is when the three of us are together. And we love to take her riding in the car; she adores it. And when I come home from lecturing, she is there waiting for me. She greets me with barks and wags, just to let me know that to her I am the most important lady in the whole world, and that no one was ever so glad to see me. Then I pat her thick fur, so soft and shiny, and I think how much I would have missed in life if I hadn't called the kennel that morning. I know that life can never again be monotonous.

She loves Bob too, and I think she shows her love better than I. At least she is more demonstrative, and she has already taken a big chunk of Bob's love in return. Sometimes I think it is he she likes the best. Around the dinner hour she will lie down by the kitchen door. Her whole being is alert as she listens for a well-known sound—the slamming of a car door and steps coming in through the garage. When Bob enters, she is right there, and what a reunion of jumping and racing, and what sweet talk! It's lucky I'm not the jealous kind, or we might have a catastrophe.

In the morning when Bob leaves, Gretchen and I look out the living-room window to see him off. I even let Gretchen put her paws up on the divan. Her tail wags fifty miles a minute and her black ears stand up straight. I wave and throw a kiss, and Bob blows a short toot on the horn. I know he is extra happy as he drives off and that he can't wait to return again to that warm, happy greeting from a man's best friend. I'm sure we wouldn't part with Gretchen for any amount of money because our home has a new warm glow since she came to stay with us.

I think that is why I said to Bob the other night, "I'm so glad we took Gretchen. We have twice as much happiness now and in a way, it seems that she has always been with us."

Bob smiled at me tenderly. "And you don't mind taking her for a walk at six o'clock every morning?"

"Not any more than you mind your walk with her the last thing at night."

Bob did not answer. He is funny that way; he doesn't want to commit himself because that was one thing he had dreaded before she came. But I know by the way they romp and the way he laughs when they come back that he doesn't mind at all.

As for me, I never knew how wide awake you become when you step outside your home before dawn, when the rest of the world seems asleep. In the eastern sky there is a touch of rose and you know that soon the sun will rise. The air is fresh and pure and now—toward winter—it is nippy and it bites my cheeks. When I return to the house and glance at myself in the mirror, my cheeks are as red as apples. It is worth the walk just to look that healthy, at least for a little while. And I feel wonderful. It is fun to put the coffeepot on, and oh, how good breakfast tastes. When we sit down to eat, Bob always asks me: "And what kind of a day is it today?"

And I give him a big smile and reply, "It is a good day, Bob, the best day that ever was and both Gretchen and I can prove that."